# DOUG LUCIE

Doug Lucie's plays include *The New Garbo* (Hull Truck, 1978),
*Heroes* (Edinburgh Festival/New End Theatre, London, 1979/80),
*Hard Feelings* (Oxford Playhouse and Bush Theatre, London,
1982), *Key to the World* (Paines Plough Lyric Hammersmith, 1984),
*Progress* (Bush, 1984; Lyric Hammersmith, 1986), *Fashion* (Royal
Shakespeare Company, Stratford and London, 1987/88; Leicester
Haymarket, 1989; Tricycle Theatre, London, 1990, which won him
a Time Out Award and Drama Magazine Best Play Award) and
*Doing the Business* (Royal Court Theatre, London, 1990).

His television credits include *Hard Feelings* and *A Class of His Own*
for the BBC in 1984, *Funseekers* (a Channel 4 film for the Comic
Strip written with Nigel Planer, 1987) and *Headhunters*, a three-part
series for BBC-1.

**Other Volumes in this Series:**

DOUG LUCIE

# GRACE

A Play

NICK HERN BOOKS
London

**A Nick Hern Book**

*Grace* first published in Great Britain in 1993 as a paperback original by
Nick Hern Books Limited, 14 Larden Road, London W3 7ST.

*Grace* copyright © 1993 by Doug Lucie

Set in Baskerville by Raven Typesetters, Ellesmere Port, South Wirral
Printed by Cox and Wyman Ltd, Reading, Berks

A CIP catalogue record for this book is available from the British Library

Doug Lucie has asserted his right to be
identified as the author of this Work.

ISBN 1-85459-245-9

For my family and all my friends who gave me so much love and support in 1992. And for everyone at Hampstead Theatre; the Libra Project, Oxford, especially, Lesley; and the staff on the Edward Buzzard Ward and the Barnes Unit, John Radcliffe Hospital, Oxford. My sincere thanks.

*Grace* was first staged at Hampstead Theatre, London on
3 December 1993.

| | |
|---|---|
| RUTH HARSTONE | Anna Massey |
| FREDDY | Ben Thomas |
| REV. NEAL HOFFMANN | James Laurenson |
| AMY HOFFMAN | Kate Fahy |
| GAVIN DRIVER | Peter Wight |
| LANCE | Kevin Dignam |
| FELICIA | Kristin Marks |
| JOANNA HOPE-COLLIER | Emma Lewis |
| *Director* | Mike Bradwell |
| *Designer* | Sue Plummer |
| *Lighting Designer* | Michael Calf |
| *Sound Designer* | John A Leonard |

*Songs by* Doug Lucie. *Arranged by* Kevin Curry

*Artistic Director*  Jenny Topper

## Characters

RUTH HARSTONE   In her fifties. An artistic English
gentlewoman.

FREDDY   In his late thirties. Of mixed race, he tends the grounds
of Hartstone.

REV NEAL HOFFMAN   In his fifties. American evangelist,
founder of Enterprise Faith, a multi-media Christian Church.

AMY HOFFMAN   In her late thirties. Neal's wife, a Christian
screenwriter.

GAVIN DRIVER   In his forties. An American-trained English
evangelist-businessman.

LANCE   In his late twenties. Driver's assistant, a zealot of the new
right.

FELICIA   In her early twenties. An American actress/singer.

JOANNA HOPE-COLLIER   In her early twenties. An English
actress, straight out of drama school.

The play takes place over a June/July weekend in the drawing
room and garden at Hartstone, a house deep in the country.

## Scene One

*The drawing room at Hartstone. Summer, early evening. RUTH is sitting at the table reading from a book into a portable tape cassette machine. She is reading from* The Water Babies.

RUTH. 'In fact, the fairies had turned him into a water baby. A water baby? You never heard of a water baby? Perhaps not. That is the very reason why this story was written. "But there are no such things as water babies." How do you know that? have you been there to see? And if you had been there to see, and had seen none, that would not prove that there were none. No one has a right to say that no water babies exist till they have seen no water babies existing; which is quite a different thing, mind, from not seeing water babies; and a thing which nobody ever did or perhaps ever will do. (*FREDDY enters through the French windows. He is mixed African/English. He wears a green shirt, fishing waistcoat, cord trousers and waders. He holds a fly fishing rod in one hand and seven or eight fresh- caught trout in the other. RUTH holds her hand up to stop him speaking and carries on reading.*) Wise men know that their business is to examine what is, and not to settle what is not.' (*She turns off the tape. FREDDY holds up the fish.*)

FREDDY. Is that enough?

RUTH. I've no idea.

FREDDY. Well how many are coming? (*Beat.*)

RUTH. Four, five, six, I don't know. Just gut them and wrap them in foil. I'll chuck them in the oven when they arrive. (*Beat.*)

FREDDY (*nodding to the book*). *The Water Babies?*

RUTH. I'm recording it for old Annie Bradley. She's blind as a bat now, poor old thing.

FREDDY. Very uplifting.

RUTH. You used to love it when you were small.

FREDDY. Yes. Except I never understood why little Tom was so ecstatic when the black washed off. (*Beat.*)

RUTH. Proper little Malcolm X, aren't we? (*Beat.*)

FREDDY (*starting to move off*). Anyway, it's definitely more than four.

RUTH. What is?

FREDDY. For dinner. The buyers.

RUTH. How do you know?

FREDDY. They were swarming all over the gatehouse as I came in. Acting like they own the place already.

RUTH. They're almost an hour early.

FREDDY (*going*). Definitely more than four, anyhow.

RUTH. You utter. . . .

*He's gone. She gets up and goes to the window and looks out. She looks alarmed, comes back to the table and picks up the book and some papers as we hear a car draw up on the gravel outside. RUTH goes off into the house.*

*Sound of car doors opening and shutting. We hear talking from offstage. GAVIN DRIVER and NEAL HOFFMAN appear, each with a shoulder bag, GAVIN with a set of plans in his hand. GAVIN walks straight in, NEAL stands in the entrance staring out into the grounds. He turns and comes into the room, smiling hugely.*

GAVIN. Did I lie?

NEAL. No, you did not. Praise the Lord. This ground is holy. I feel it.

*AMY HOFFMAN comes in. She is pale and drawn. She goes straight to the table and sits, taking out a small bottle of mineral water and some pills. She swallows one.*

How you feeling, honey? (*She pulls a face.*) Maybe take a nap later . . .

GAVIN (*goes to the door and shouts*). Hello?! Miss Hartstone?

NEAL. Gavin, Amy has a headache . . .

GAVIN. Sorry, Neal . . .

AMY. I have an inner-ear imbalance . . .

NEAL. Whatever . . .

AMY. It's a whole different thing . . .

NEAL. You had a headache in the car . . .

AMY. I felt *dizzy* in the car . . .

FREDDY *comes in.*

GAVIN. Ah, Freddy, Hello, is Ruth about?

FREDDY. She's in the kitchen. She'll be up in a minute. D'you need a hand with the bags?

GAVIN. That's very kind.

FREDDY. No problem.   *(He goes out to the car.)*

NEAL. Who in the heck is that?

GAVIN. That's Freddy. He looks after the place.

FELICIA, JOANNA *and* LANCE *appear.* LANCE *carries cases.*

FELICIA. Some place . . .

JOANNA. I bet it's a fridge in winter.

FELICIA. So, this is where it happened, huh?

GAVIN. Right here.

FELICIA. Neat.

NEAL *is holding his arms out.*

GAVIN. Just leave them there for now, Lance.

LANCE *puts the cases down.*

NEAL. Brothers and sisters . . . (*They all assume a solumn, prayerful attitude.*) . . . Let us pray. Lord, we thank you for your guidance and protection in bringing us safely to our destination. We thank you for shining your light in the darkness to lead us to this holy place. This place from which we will expand our mission of spiritual enlightenment. This place of miracles.

FREDDY *comes in with some cases.*

Thank you Lord. Amen.

ALL. Amen.

FREDDY. That's all the bags.

GAVIN. Thanks, Freddy. Oh, everyone, this is Freddy. And Freddy, this is the Reverend Neal Hoffman.

NEAL. God bless you brother.

GAVIN. . . . His wife Amy, Felicia, Joanna and Lance. (*They say hello, wave, etc*).

FREDDY. So. Good journey?

GAVIN. Yes, we made very good time.

NEAL. The Lord cleared a path to expedite our arrival. (FREDDY's *not sure how to take this*.)

FREDDY. Good. (*Beat*.) Uh, shall I show you the rooms?

GAVIN. Yes, would you? I think the ladies might want to freshen up a little.

FREDDY. OK. It's this way. (*The women follow him off*.)

GAVIN. You might like to take the cases up, Lance . . .

LANCE. Oh, sure. (*He picks up some cases and goes, leaving* NEAL *and* GAVIN *alone*.)

GAVIN. Well.

NEAL. Well yourself. (*They smile*.) And *is* it a fridge in winter?

GAVIN. It won't be. Not with central heating. Don't worry, it's all in the conversion budget.

NEAL. Uh huh. So what do these people do for heat?

GAVIN. Don't laugh, but they wear lots of woollens. They put on three jumpers, throw plenty of logs on the fire and huddle together in one room.

NEAL. Real pioneer spirit. I think our pilgrims will be expecting hot and cold running, however.

GAVIN. And they shall have it.

NEAL. Praise the Lord.

GAVIN. Amen.

NEAL. OK, that land on the right, as we drove up to the house . . . that part of the estate?

GAVIN. All of it. Everything you can see, and then some. (*He spreads out the plans on the table and points to various parts*.) This is the section you saw. That'll be the campsite. And down this way . . . (*He points out into the grounds*.) . . . that's where we'll put up the church marquee. I'll take you down there later. And that whole front area where we drove in, there we have space for 1,000 cars, with optional space on the upper pasture for another five hundred.

LANCE *comes back in and picks up more cases.*

NEAL. Everything OK?

LANCE. Mrs Hoffman changed your room, the first one was South . . .

NEAL. South facing, yeah.

LANCE. Apart from that, everything's fine. And I think this place is absolutely brilliant.

*They smile. He goes.*

NEAL. Fine boy.

GAVIN. Yes, absolutely first class. Very committed.

NEAL. Now, how about these outhouses and stuff we're going to convert?

GAVIN. Ah, they're out this way, down towards the river. It's a beautiful spot.

NEAL. Can't wait to see it.

GAVIN. I can show you round the estate before dinner, if you're not too tired.

NEAL. Never too tired to do God's work, Gavin.

GAVIN. Amen.

*NEAL breaks away, smiling, and inspects the room.*

NEAL. I feel a permanence here. It's real.

*RUTH appears at the french windows and stares off in the direction of the limousine.*

GAVIN. Ah, Ruth.

RUTH. What a most extraordinary motorcar.

NEAL *(chuckles)*. It's a Mercedes stretch limousine.

RUTH. Good grief. Is it yours? It must have cost a fortune.

NEAL. The Lord has been very generous to my automotive needs.

RUTH. How awfully good of him. *(Beat.)* You must be Gavin's partner.

NEAL. Correction, his boss. Reverend Neal Hoffman. Honoured to meet you, Miss Hartstone. *(He shakes her hand.)*

RUTH. Yes . . .

NEAL. The house is more beautiful than I ever imagined.

RUTH. Yes, lovely, isn't it? The old place is falling to bits,
  mind . . .

NEAL. That's history, Miss Hartstone.

RUTH. Do please call me Ruth.

NEAL. Things decay only for the Lord to build them up again,
  Ruth.

RUTH. He deals in motor cars *and* does building repairs. Gosh.
  Or am I being too literal? (NEAL *smiles*.)

NEAL. When you've been slain in the spirit, anything is possible
  with the Lord.

RUTH. Really?

NEAL. John, three, three. 'Except a man be born again, he cannot
  see the kingdom of God.'

RUTH. Oh, I see. He's a sort of spiritual freemason.

NEAL. Except everybody can join.

RUTH. It would appear they're obliged to, if they want to get
  anywhere.

GAVIN. You're wasting your time Neal. I'm afraid Ruth's just an
  old fashioned sceptic.

NEAL. You're not like your sister, then?

RUTH. Not at all like my sister, no.

NEAL. That's a real shame.

RUTH. Is it? She died aged fifteen. I'm still here. I think I can
  confidently say I got the better deal.

NEAL. She didn't die, Ruth, she didn't die.

RUTH. Sorry to contradict you, but I saw them carry her body
  away. I kissed her in the coffin. She was cold. (*Beat.*) But I
  understand what you mean.

NEAL. I still can't quite believe I'm standing where it happened.

RUTH. What did?

NEAL. Grace. Your sister. Where she passed over.

RUTH. Oh. Well, if you want to be strictly accurate she actually popped her clogs in her room upstairs.

GAVIN. Yes, we were hoping to conduct a service up there, as a matter of fact.

NEAL. A thanksgiving. For a short but miraculous life. (*Beat.*)

RUTH. Be my guest. It's a bit of a broom cupboard, though. I doubt you'll all fit in.

GAVIN. We'll manage. (*Beat.*)

RUTH. Well, let me offer you a sherry.

GAVIN. Lovely, thank you. (*She goes to the drinks and pours three sherries.*)

NEAL. So, Ruth, is Freddy all the workforce you employ now?

RUTH. Freddy doesn't work for me, he *lives* here. I don't have anybody working for me any more.

NEAL. I guess not. My motto, Ruth: let the businessman get on with business. We know how to look after people. And I reckon the people round here deserve a few breaks after the mess you got them in to.

RUTH. We . . . did our best.

NEAL. Well I've been in business twenty five years, and good intentions are fine things to have, but they don't guarantee a profit and a paycheck.

RUTH. Our failure was hardly unique.

NEAL. But you made elementary mistakes, if you don't mind me saying so. I mean, you went into production with an untested product; you borrowed way past your ability to pay back; you didn't lay people off when you should have. And worst, you didn't research your market. If you had, you'd have discovered there wasn't a demand for your jam.

RUTH. High-class organic preserves, actually.

NEAL. Whatever. (*Beat.*) The fact is, Ruth, you tried to sell a product nobody needed.

RUTH. But I thought that was the basis of the entire system.

NEAL. And as a consequence, the good people around here who'd put their faith in you were dragged down along with you.

RUTH. They knew there were risks. Nobody was coerced.

NEAL. And you owe the banks an awful lot of money.

RUTH. But you're here to put that right.

NEAL. Correct. (*Beat.*)

RUTH. You've certainly been doing your homework on us.

NEAL. You can bet we have. (*Beat.*) And tell me, did Gavin show you the 'Grace' screenplay?

RUTH. He did, yes.

NEAL. And how did you find it? (*Beat.*)

RUTH. Fascinating.

GAVIN. We've obviously taken a few liberties, you know . . .

RUTH. Feel free. Artistic licence, and all that.

NEAL. But I think you'll have to agree, it's jam packed with spirituality.

RUTH. Oh, jam packed. Absolutely.

NEAL. Amy, that's my wife, she wrote the script.

RUTH. Yes, I'm very much looking forward to meeting her. I've just been reading some of her short stories. (*Beat.*)

NEAL. She, uh, won't thank you for bringing that up.

RUTH. Why ever not?

GAVIN. They were written before she was born again.

RUTH. So? (*Beat.*)

NEAL. They were the work of the Devil, Ruth. (*Beat.*) And the Devil wants your soul. He wants my soul, too, but you better believe it, he's gonna have a war on his hands if he tries to get it.

RUTH. I see.

NEAL. Because I'm with the Lord.

GAVIN. Amen.

RUTH. Another sherry, anyone?

NEAL. No, thank you. (*Beat.*) I need to freshen up a little before dinner.

RUTH. Of course. We eat at eight. Informal. No need to dress.

NEAL. Thank you, ma'am. (*He looks at his watch.*) Gavin, what do you say we take that walk at seven thirty?

GAVIN. Seven thirty it is. I'll come and get you.

NEAL. Fine. Ruth.

RUTH. Reverend.

*He goes.* RUTH *pours a sherry.*

Tell me, Gavin . . . would I be right in thinking that the Reverend Hoffman is just ever so slightly bonkers?

GAVIN (*laughs*). Ever so slightly American would probably be nearer the mark.

RUTH. I've known plenty of Americans. But never one quite like the Reverend.

GAVIN. That's because he's a true Christian, Ruth. (*Beat.*) Us Brits, you see, we're brought up to see some virtue in quiet, reserve, the stiff upper lip. Even when we discover Jesus we've been loath to shout out the good news. Whereas our American cousins have no such inhibitions. They believe that good news is worth spreading. If you don't holler it out at the top of your lungs, you're letting the Lord down.

RUTH. Doesn't that presuppose that the rest of us are all deaf?

GAVIN. Can you be so sure that you're not?

RUTH. Excuse me, Gavin, my family were missionaries. I was clubbed senseless with the word of God from the tender age of two. I am not deaf. I stopped listening. (*Beat.*)

GAVIN. Sorry.

RUTH. Don't be. Just don't try to convert me. I've been there and back again and the trip was most definitely not worth it.

GAVIN. You know . . . something I realised very early in life: that scepticism is a darn sight easier than belief.

RUTH. Gavin, please understand . . . God, Jesus, the Devil, all that . . . I find it very painful, that's all. (*Beat.*) Well, if you'll excuse me, I believe I've got a lot of trout to gut, otherwise we shall all go hungry.

GAVIN. Well, we can't have that.

JOANNA *comes in.*

Ah, Ruth, before you go, let me introduce you. This is Joanna Hope-Collier. Joanna, this is Miss Hartstone.

JOANNA. Crumbs, hello . . .

RUTH. Hello . . .

JOANNA. I'm playing you. You know, as a young girl. In the film.

RUTH. Well. I hope you have more luck with it than I did.

*She goes.*

JOANNA. Did I say something stupid?

GAVIN. No.

JOANNA. Shit, I bet I did. (*Beat.*) Oops, sorry.

GAVIN. Profanity is totally unnecessary at any time.

JOANNA. Sorry. (*Beat.*) Incredible place, isn't it?

GAVIN. Yes.

JOANNA. I mean . . . so historic. (*Beat.*) That black bloke showed us the room where Grace died, where Jesus appeared. Just a little bed and a table.

GAVIN. I cried. When I first stepped into that room I felt the physical presence of the Lord and I wept for joy.

JOANNA. Amazing.

GAVIN. Yes. (*Beat.*)  Where's Felicia?

JOANNA. Taking a nap. She's still jet-lagged.

GAVIN. Make sure she's up in time for dinner.

JOANNA. Yuh. (*Beat.*) Any news on your wife?

GAVIN. No. We just have to pray that the baby can wait until after this weekend.

JOANNA. What if it doesn't? Will you have to go back to London?

GAVIN. I can't possibly. Not until those contracts have Ruth's signature on them. (*Beat.*) I was there for the births of the other four. I can hardly be called uncaring.

JOANNA. Hardly that.

LANCE *comes in.*

LANCE. Joanna, there you are.

JOANNA. Oh, hello, Lance.

LANCE. Been looking all over for you. A guy could get well and truly lost in this place, I tell you. They've stuck me out in the West wing or whatever you call it. The bathroom's route march distance.

JOANNA. I'm much closer.

LANCE. Yeah, lucky beggar. Still, quite a thrill to be here at all, eh, Gavin?

GAVIN. Yes, quite a thrill.

LANCE. The old order. They had it easy all right. Still, que sera. Our turn now. (*He and* GAVIN *smile.*) And all done without a single shot being fired.

GAVIN. Amen. (*Beat.*)

LANCE. Jo, fancy a poke about? Explore the place?

JOANNA. OK. Oh, I just have to ask Gavin something. You go on, I'll catch up with you.

LANCE. Righto.

*He goes out.*

GAVIN. I think Lance has taken rather a shine to you.

JOANNA. I think so too. (*Beat.*)

GAVIN. What did you want to ask me? (*Beat.*)

JOANNA. Oh . . . should I come to your room tonight? Later? (*Beat.*)

GAVIN. Sometimes when I look at you, I shake. I try not to, but something takes me over. Forgive me. (*Beat.*)

JOANNA. Shall I? (*Beat.*)

GAVIN. Please.

JOANNA. Thanks.

*She goes out.*

GAVIN. Thanks.

*Blackout. On speakers* FELICIA's *recording of 'He is the Cord' is heard:*
'There's someone up there caring, watching from above.
You may not have met him, but you know his name is love.

He watches daily over us, he keeps us all from fear
For he is all around us now, he is everywhere.'


## Scene Two

*After dinner, about 10.00 p.m. FELICIA is in the centre of the room
playing an acoustic guitar and singing 'He is the Cord'. Watching are
AMY, JOANNA, LANCE and FREDDY.*

FELICIA (*Singing*).
 He is the light, he is the might.
 He is the man, his is the hand.
 He is the Lord, he is the cord,
 That binds us to eternal life.

 *She exhorts the others to join in the reprise of this final chorus. All but
 FREDDY join in. FELICIA finishes on a big flourish. The others clap,
 LANCE whoops American style. FELICIA claps and whoops.*

FELICIA (*cries out with joy*). OK! Right! OK!

AMY. Praise the Lord.

FELICIA. Amen. (*To FREDDY.*) Well? How'd you like it?

FREDDY. Great. Thanks.

FELICIA. You're welcome. That song's what we call 'easy
 listening inspirational', but on the album I really get to rock out.
 That's why it's called 'Rowdy Worship'.

FREDDY. I'd like to hear it some time.

 *FELICIA takes a cassette tape from her bag and hands it to him.*

FELICA. OK, you got it. Here you go. Don't worry, I have plenty
 of copies.

FREDDY. Thanks a lot.

FELICIA. You're welcome.

FREDDY (*looking at the tape*). Have you sold many?

FELICIA. That album you have in your hand there has sold 250
 thousand units and still climbing. Watch out, people, the
 electronic Gospel is coming to save the world, hallelujah.

FREDDY. I never knew it was such big business.

LANCE. Mega. Absolutely ginormous.

FELICIA. You talk the rock'n'roll faith thing, you're talking growth. See, people want the music to plug into their belief systems.

FREDDY. Is that right?

LANCE. And do you know what the catalyst was? What started it all off?

FREDDY. Let me see . . . Gospel music?

FELICIA. No, that was just, you know, for black folks.

LANCE. What started it off was Jesus Christ Superstar. (*Beat.*) No kid. Another Brit triumph.

FELICIA. The Reverend started up Enterprise Faith Records after he saw the show. Isn't that right, Amy?

AMY. That's correct.

FELICIA. Christian ethics in today's musical idiom is how he describes it.

FREDDY. You mean you appropriated modern secular musical forms to propagate your specifically religious message.

FELICIA. I guess . . .

AMY. You got it.

FREDDY. Very clever.

AMY. We discovered a product gap and filled it, to the glory of the Lord. That's all.

FREDDY. Well, nice one, as they say. (*Beat.*)

JOANNA. I am totally cream crackered. Anybody mind if I hit the sack?

AMY. Not at all, honey.

LANCE (*Standing*). Find your way OK?

JOANNA. I should think so. Goodnight. (*They all 'goodnight'. She goes.*)

FELICIA. Uh, excuse me, what is cream crackered?

LANCE. Cream crackered, knackered. Er, bushed, beat.

FELICIA. Oh . . .

AMY. Cockney rhyming slang, that right?

LANCE. That's right.

FELICIA. Joanna's a cockney?

LANCE. No. People of her class sometimes use the slang. They find the incongruity what they call 'a bit of a wheeze', apparently.

FELICIA. Cute.

LANCE. Yeah. (*Beat.*)

FREDDY. So . . . let me get this right . . . Joanna's playing Ruth, in the film. . .

FELICIA. Right.

FREDDY. And you're playing Grace. . .

FELICIA. Right. Hey, don't worry, I have a voice coach.

FREDDY. I'm sure you'll be wonderful.

NEAL, RUTH *and* GAVIN *appear from the grounds, mid-conversation.*

FELICIA. Thank you.

NEAL. . . . and of course, something many people don't know is that the word 'evangelical' comes from the Greek, meaning good news. Did you know that Ruth?

RUTH. Yes I did as a matter of fact.

GAVIN. Can you excuse me for a minute, Neal? I have to call the clinic, check on Sophie.

NEAL. Take your time. And hey, be sure to tell that little lady we all love her and we're all praying for her.

GAVIN. I'll do that.

*He goes outside and talks into his mobile phone.* NEAL *flops down into a chair and undoes his tie.*

NEAL. Lance, you have those visitor projections ready for me?

LANCE. Uh, yeah, I think so. You want them now?

NEAL. First thing tomorrow.

LANCE. I'd better go over them now, then.

NEAL. That would be much appreciated.

LANCE. OK. (*He gets up.*)

NEAL (*To* FELICIA.) And you, little lady, you get your beauty sleep. I don't want any wrinkles showing up on that film. OK?

FELICIA. Yes sir. Goodnight.

NEAL. And God bless.

*She and* LANCE *go.*

And you honey? Tired?

AMY. I guess so.

NEAL. OK then. (*They kiss.*) Sleep tight.

AMY. Goodnight everybody. (*She goes*).

RUTH. Just how many people are we expecting for this filming on Sunday?

NEAL. Only two or three, it's not a full shoot. We're making a trailer for transmission on our TV station back home, then our viewers send in their donations, and we've raised the cost of our movie.

RUTH. I see.

NEAL. I hope you'll come along and watch. We'd be joyed to have you.

RUTH. I may do that. (*Beat.*) I must say, I'm amazed at the way the youngsters do exactly as you tell them. That's very rare these days.

NEAL. Self-discipline. One of the first things you learn when you're with The Lord. Without it, you're nothing, nobody. Take me, Ruth, I didn't always walk in God's light. You may not know, but I was brought up in poverty. I never knew my father. He left before I was born. And my mother was an alcoholic, so I was raised mostly in institutions and foster homes. (*Beat.*) I may look to you now like a respectable old clergyman, but I was a real wild young man for a time. Oh yes. You know how it was. Change the world, equality, peace, drugs, free living, I bought the whole store.

RUTH. Well, we all did some very strange things in those days. Take me, I married a plumber. Name of Brian.

NEAL. Really?

RUTH. Yes. He fixed all my taps then disappeared to Amsterdam with a Moroccan stilt-walker.

NEAL. Well. (*Beat.*) I didn't realise at the time, but what I had was a hunger. I swallowed everything . . . booze, grass, acid, and still I was starving. I had no father to respect; I had no respect for anything or anybody, myself included. I ran around spitting hatred everywhere, round and round, confused, angry and deeply, deeply unhappy.

RUTH. And then, don't tell me, you found God.

NEAL. No, Ruth, no. What I'd found was the Devil. (*Beat.*) He spoke to me. I went around in a dream for I don't know how long, with the Devil speaking to me, on and on and on. And do you know what he was saying? (*Beat.*) He was telling me to kill. Yes, to kill. So I went out and I bought a gun. I didn't know who I was going to kill, it could have been the President, it could have been the check-out girl at the K-mart. (*Beat.*) But I found myself in a huge stadium. I didn't know why I was there, what was going on, I only knew I had to kill. Surrounded by thousands of people, but who? And then I knew. There he was, framed in lights. There was the man I was going to kill. (*Beat.*) Dr Billy Graham. (*Beat.*) I had my hand on the gun in my jacket pocket as I pressed forward to get close enough. And the Devil was screaming at me, and Billy was preaching, and I had these voices, yelling and hollering, fighting for my soul. And Billy was telling us to come forward to Jesus, and I was going forward, and I had the gun in my hand. And at last I stood before him. And I was shaking, Lord I was shaking. And then I looked up. (*Beat.*) And the Devil was gone. No more yelling in my head. For the very first time in my life, I felt peace. Complete, silent, loving peace. So I tore off my jacket and threw it way behind me. I fell to my knees. And I said, 'Dr Graham, forgive me, but I came here to kill you.' And he smiled, and fell to his knees and we prayed together. (*Beat.*) A miracle. (*Beat.*) And that was when I understood. It was me that had to change first. Only then could I change the world.

RUTH. Rather like St Paul.

NEAL. Yes! Precisely. Just as it happened in the Bible, so, two thousand years later, it happened to me. Isn't that just incredible?

RUTH. Oh, incredible.

NEAL. You see, God's purpose never ever changes. From the time of the Scriptures to now, the message is the same: reject the Devil and come to the Lord. (*Beat.*)

RUTH. The problem I have, Reverend, is that in my entire life, I have never had any inkling of the existence of God. Or the Devil. I can accept, for the sake of argument, that they exist, but then that acceptance brings with it a question: if they are constantly struggling for possession of the soul of humankind, then why have so very many people, myself included, never had any sign of this titanic struggle raging all around us?

NEAL. I expect they were trying to get through, but I'll bet your line was always busy.

RUTH. No. It's not deliberate on my part. If God were to manifest Himself to me I shouldn't complain. In fact, I would be grateful for some answers. (*Beat.*) It's just that it will never happen, that's all. (*Beat.*)

NEAL. God's love is there, Ruth. You've chosen to ignore it.

RUTH. So it's my fault.

NEAL. Of course. That's why you're so unhappy. That's why you're having to sell this place. Without the Lord, there is no happiness or success. There is only the saddest state in the world: Godlessness. The endless black eternity of living without his love.

FREDDY. And why, specifically, should eternity be black?

NEAL (*He laughs*). A figure of speech, brother, a figure of speech.

FREDDY. Yes, it always is.

NEAL. Black like the night is black.

FREDDY. And where does, say, poverty rate on this sliding scale of sadness?

NEAL. Very high indeed. You should read your Bible, brother. The poor man who accepts Jesus Christ into his heart possesses all the riches of the kingdom of God.

FREDDY (*exploding with laughter*). Oh, man, you are priceless! It's just words, for Christ's sake. (*He stalks out.*)

RUTH. Freddy . . . (*Pause.*) Sorry.

NEAL. That's OK, Ruth. A lot of people get sentimental about poverty. (*Beat.*) If he cares so darn much, why isn't he out there doing something about it like I am?

RUTH. I wasn't aware you were a philanthropist. I was under the impression that you were a businessman, somebody who looks to make a profit.

NEAL. I'm a Christian businessman. Every cent I earn goes to the glory of God. And that employs people, that puts bread on the table, that gives people hope.

RUTH. It's also given you that enormous limousine outside and that lovely Rolex on your wrist.

NEAL. The Lord has blessed me in kind. He has chosen to reward me financially because I've put to use my God-given business talent. (*Beat.*)

RUTH. So there really *is* an answer for everything.

NEAL. Yes. God is the answer.

RUTH. I'm sorry, but I believe that anybody who thinks God is the answer has seriously misunderstood the question.

GAVIN *comes back in.*

GAVIN. Well. Sophie sends you her love, Neal.

NEAL. God bless her. How is she?

GAVIN. Bearing up. But nothing's happening as yet, so we can get right on with business.

RUTH. Yes. You were going to show me your brochure. All the exciting things you intend doing with my home. (*Beat.*) Ex-home.

GAVIN. It's still yours for at least a couple of months.

RUTH. I shall be glad to be rid of it.

GAVIN. No, I can't believe that.

RUTH. Oh, believe it. And the two million pounds you're paying me for it has seen off any lingering doubts I may have had.

GAVIN (*having taken a large glossy brochure out of his case*). Here we are.

RUTH. It's very professional looking.

NEAL. What did you expect?

RUTH (*reading the cover*). 'Hartstone. Christian leisure and satellite broadcasting complex. Hartstone: Retreat. Church. Shrine. Hartstone: The truly Christian experience.' Hmm. I suppose in a year or two I won't recognise the place.

GAVIN. Apart from the obvious building and alteration work we'll have to undertake, we've gone to great lengths to retain the essential character of the place.

RUTH. Don't worry. The essential character went long ago. It's all yours.

NEAL. Ruth . . . I love this place.

RUTH (*holding up the brochure*). No. You love *this* place.

NEAL. Same thing. (*Beat.*)

RUTH. No. (*Pause. She looks through the brochure.*) I must say, I'm intrigued to know how you got planning permission for some of this. I mean, aren't we an area of special scientific intrest, or some such? I should have thought the DOE would have tied you up in red tape. (GAVIN *smiles.*) Or am I mistaken?

GAVIN. We have satisfied every aspect of government concern, I think you could say.

RUTH. Oh. You went to school with the minister.

GAVIN. Not quite. But I have done a little consultancy work for the government in the past. I have very good contacts.

NEAL. But don't think this is achieved by graft, Ruth. The government wants the same thing we want for this area: jobs and prosperity.

GAVIN. And we really have bent over backwards to accommodate the Green lobby and the inevitable local nimbies.

NEAL. So, everybody's happy. (*Beat.*) Uh, let me see if I can't offer a little something that might make *you* even happier Ruth. How would you like to stay on here? (*Beat.*) I happen to believe there is a role here for you at Hartstone after we take over.

RUTH. Doing what?

NEAL. Bearing witness. Telling our visitors the fantastic story of your family and Grace in particular. Showing them round the place, giving them the true picture of life as it was for you here back then. (*Beat.*)

RUTH. There are a few things I feel I may have been cut out for in life, Reverend, but I'm afraid Redcoat isn't one of them.

NEAL. Excuse me?

RUTH. I'd make a lousy spiritual tour guide.

NEAL. What the heck has that got to do with the Redcoats?

GAVIN. I'll explain another time, Neal.

NEAL. You people have got to stop talking in riddles. (*Looks at his watch.*) Well, my lovely Rolex tells me it's time I got some sleep. What time's our first meeting tomorrow?

GAVIN. The contractors will be here at ten, then it's pretty solid through the day.

NEAL. That's how I like it.

FREDDY *comes back in.*

FREDDY. Sorry. I shouldn't have blown up like that.

NEAL. Thank you, brother. Apology accepted. (*Beat.*) OK. Sleep. God bless you all. (*He goes.*)

GAVIN. Looks like I missed something.

RUTH. The merest altercation.

GAVIN. Ah. (*Beat.*) By the way, Ruth, Neal just threw *me* a curve there as well.

RUTH. I'm sorry?

GAVIN. Staying on. I know it wouldn't appeal to you.

RUTH. No.

GAVIN. He can be rather impulsive at times, but, you know, next to Billy Graham, Neal is the most . . . inspirational man I ever met. Do you know about his conversion? How it came about?

RUTH. Yes, it was in the literature you sent me. And, oddly enough, we were just treated to a word for word rendition of it while you were out. Luckily, I got in with St Paul before he could reach the finale. (*Beat.*)

GAVIN. Well. We all love him very dearly, despite his little foibles.

RUTH. Unfortunately, he reminds me of my father.

GAVIN. Is that unfortunate?

RUTH. In as much as I hated my father, yes.

GAVIN. That is very sad.

RUTH. Why?

GAVIN. Well . . . we believe that manliness is Christliness; that much sorrow and pain has been caused by women refusing to accept the authority of their fathers and husbands. (*Beat.*)

RUTH. Which century precisely is it, Gavin, to which you would drag us back?

GAVIN. We simply go back to the Bible.

RUTH. Very convenient.

GAVIN. There's nothing convenient about it at all. It's the word of God and must be obeyed, that's all.

RUTH. I wonder how enthusiastically you'd obey if it turned out not to suit you so very well. (*Beat.*)

GAVIN. I forget, your mind's made up about us already.

RUTH. Long, long ago.

GAVIN. Well, I'll pray for God to open your mind and enter your heart.

RUTH. Please, don't bother.

GAVIN. It's no bother. (*He smiles.*) Right, well, I'll get off to bed, too. Big day tomorrow. Goodnight, and God bless. (*He goes*).

*Pause.* RUTH *gets her copy of The Water Babies and sets up the cassette machine.*

RUTH. You shouldn't get so worked up.

FREDDY. Me? (*Beat.*) It's just that they're such . . . bastards. Sorry.

RUTH. Feel free. Very soon, they'll own the world. (*Beat.*) Those poor innocent souls in Gdansk, Bucharest, Vladivostock . . . they won't know what's hit them. The joys of the free market, and in less than one year, the Reverend Hoffman beamed into their homes via satellite, twenty four hours a day. Makes you shudder, doesn't it? (*Beat.*) Forget the rubbish about the meek inheriting the earth. This bunch are buying it up in one job lot.

FREDDY. (*Beat.*) And you're not going to tell them the truth. You know . . .

RUTH. No. Why should I?

FREDDY. Because it's dishonest.

RUTH. This is England. Nobody is honest any more. There's no return on honesty. (*Pause.*) Have you seen what they're going to do to your river?

FREDDY. He told me.

RUTH. No, look, there's an artist's impression of it here. (*She hands him the brochure.*) Hideous, isn't it?

FREDDY. Don't.

RUTH. A marina, boating, water skiing.

FREDDY. Yes . . .

RUTH. 'A total riverside leisure environment.' It says here.

FREDDY (*Beat*). It's obscene. They're going to kill that river. For money.

RUTH. Welcome to the real world. (*Beat.*)

FREDDY. I won't forgive you, you know.

RUTH. Look . . . They've made a film about the Apostles. Available only on video, it says. A film about the Apostles entitled 'The Magnificent Twelve'. (*Beat.*) No sensible God would allow his followers to be so idiotic, surely.

FREDDY. It's not a joke.

RUTH. I'm afraid the jury's still out on that one.

FREDDY. Oh, I know, disguise it with irony, as per usual. But the pain in this house is real. *My* pain is real.

RUTH (*reading from the brochure*). 'Enterprise Faith is at the forefront of the major revival of the Church in Europe – East and West. We are putting the Church into the marketplace. We are changing the hearts and minds of *people*. That's where the revival begins. That is the Gospel of Faith. Enterprise Faith.' (*Pause.* FREDDY *stands to go.*) Freddy I have no desire to be forgiven anything.

FREDDY. I'm going to the river.

RUTH ( *throws the brochure and opens the book and switches on the tape recorder. She reads out loud*). ' "And now, my pretty little man," said Mother Carey, "you are sure you know the way to the Other-end-of-Nowhere?" Tom thought; and behold, he had forgotten it utterly. "That is because you took your eyes off me." "But what am I to do, ma'am? For I can't keep looking at you when I am somewhere else." "You must do without me, as most people have to do, and of course, you must go the whole way backward." "Backward!" cried Tom, "Then I shall not be able

to see my way." "On the contrary, if you look forward, you will
not see a step before you, and be certain to go wrong; but, if you
look behind you, and watch carefully whatever you have passed,
then you will know what is coming next as plainly as if you saw
it in a looking glass." '

## Scene Three

*Saturday morning 11.00 a.m.* FELICIA *and* JOANNA *are rehearsing a
scene from the film. This is not immediately obvious, although* FELICIA *is
trying to speak with an English accent, because their scripts are on the table.*

FELICIA. Do you ever wonder what Heaven must be like?

JOANNA. Sometimes.

FELICIA. And what do you think?

JOANNA. Oh, I expect it's very light and warm . . . with nice
trees for shade and cool streams, and everybody happy. Yes, lots
of singing and laughing . . . (*Pause. She's forgotten the line.*
FELICIA *prompts.*)

FELICIA. How about you?

JOANNA. Shit, sorry. (*Beat.*) How about you?

FELICIA. Oh . . . I think of Heaven as being cradled in God's
bosom . . . a deep warm feeling, with His strong arms around
me. And Jesus there, smiling. A smile like all the nicest things in
the world. A smile like healing medicine. (*She coughs badly.*
JOANNA *goes to her.*)

JOANNA. You're going to be all right. I've been praying for you.
You're going to be well again, soon.

FELICIA. I don't mind, you know. I'm not afraid to die, if it's the
Lord's will.

JOANNA. You're so brave. (*Beat.*) Uh . . . no, I've lost my
objective, sorry. (*She goes and consults her script.*)

FELICIA. That's OK. (*Beat.*) You think I need to work on the
cough?

JOANNA. No, it sounds really . . . death rattle, you know?

FELICIA. Thank you. Hey, I can't wait till we get our costumes.

We can just hang out, and, like, really become Grace and Ruth.

JOANNA. Yeah, dead method. (*Beat.*) God, I hope they didn't wear corsets.

FELICIA. Uh uh, too young.

JOANNA. I wore one once in a telly I did. Nearly killed me. (*Beat.*) Maybe they wore suspenders.

FELICIA. Suspenders?

FREDDY *comes in from the grounds carrying a shotgun.*

JOANNA. Oh, hello.

FREDDY. Hello.

FELICIA. Shoot anything?

FREDDY. No.

JOANNA. Good. Dead things, yuk.

FREDDY (*he laughs.*) You eat meat?

JOANNA. Yeah. But . . .

FREDDY. Humanely slaughtered, right? My favourite contradiction. Dead is dead, whichever way you look at it.

JOANNA. At least my dinner's been killed for a reason. It hasn't been killed for fun.

FREDDY. I have never in my life killed anything for fun. (*Beat.*) Bye. (*He smiles and goes.*)

JOANNA. Guns give me the creeps, that's all.

FELICIA. Every man has the right to defend himself.

JOANNA. Against what? Rabbits? (*Beat.*)

FELICIA. I guess we're just a lot more comfortable around guns in the States.

JOANNA. Well I hate them.

FELICIA. I grew up with them. My daddy has a real big collection. And he always says it ain't the bullet that kills you, it's the hole.

JOANNA. What a cop out.

FELICIA. Why? Any how, I think Freddy looks kinda neat with a gun.

JOANNA. Whoah, I get it.

FELICIA. Get what?

JOANNA. You know . . .

FELICIA. What?

JOANNA. You've got the hots for Freddy.

FELICIA *looks angry*.

FELICIA. No, I do not. That's not right.

JOANNA. I'm sorry. Just a joke.

FELICIA. Yeah. (*Beat.*)

JOANNA. You're not . . . I mean . . . don't be offended . . . you're not prejudiced, are you? (FELICIA *is furious*.)

FELICIA. No. How dare you say that?

JOANNA. Sorry.

FELICIA. How dare you? (*Pause.*)

JOANNA. Look, uh, I've got a big mouth, OK? I don't always check my brain's in gear when I open it. Sorry.

FELICIA. I had a Negro boyfriend, as a matter of fact.

JOANNA. Oh. (*Beat.*)

FELICIA. He's a real great guy. A real strong Christian. He works at Faith records, we met when I was cutting the album. (*Beat.*) My mom thought Bob, that's his name, she thought Bob was a great guy, the best, she told me so. But when I told her I was in love she said she'd been praying that this wouldn't happen. She'd been praying. (*Beat.*) And we couldn't tell my Daddy. Daddy wouldn't have understood. (*Beat.*) And folks at Faith, well, they were kind of weird about it, too. Bad career choice was how Reverend Hoffman put it. (*Beat.*) We never fooled around, nothing like that. We were just a good Christian couple. But we had kind of an acceptance problem. (*Beat.*)

JOANNA. Do you still see him?

FELICIA. Not really. (*Upset, she goes to her bag and takes out her walkman.*)

JOANNA. Funny place, your country.

FELICIA. Yeah, real funny. (AMY *comes in.*)

AMY. Hi.

FELICIA }
JOANNA } Hi

FELICIA. Sleep OK?

AMY. More or less . . .

FELICIA. So how you feeling?

AMY. Better, you know . . . a little bit dizzy at times . . .

FELICIA. Take it easy.

AMY. Yeah.

> FELICIA *is preparing to listen to her walkman.*

> You kids been out yet? Round the property?

JOANNA. I had a look round last night. It's fantastic.

FELICIA. I just need a scripture moment. Excuse me.

AMY. Go right ahead.

> FELICIA *puts on her headphones and closes her eyes. As she listens, she sometimes sits swaying gently, sometimes paces around with her hands clasped.*

JOANNA. What's she doing?

AMY. She's taking a spiritual supplement. (*Beat.*) It's a two minute reading from the scriptures. So, you're stuck in traffic, or doing the laundry, or waiting on line at the bank, and you feel what we call Bible hunger, you just put in the tape, close your eyes and get filled right up with the word of God.

> FELICIA *is nodding her head and occasionally saying amen.*

JOANNA. You're kidding.

AMY. No.

JOANNA (*laughing*). Like taking an aspirin.

AMY. Except the word of God brings greater relief and comfort than aspirin ever could. (*Beat.*)

JOANNA. Felicia was telling me about Bob . . .

AMY. Oh yeah?

JOANNA. Yeah. I think it got her a bit upset.

AMY. Well, y'know, it can be pretty distressing when a guy, y'know, when a relationship breaks down one side. She got awful hurt.

JOANNA. What, you're saying he dumped her?

AMY. Uh, well, I guess . . . well, yeah. (*Beat.*)

JOANNA. So it had nothing to do with his colour.

AMY. Excuse me?

JOANNA. She seemed to think it might have had something to do with . . . well, y'know.

AMY. No.

JOANNA. He's black.

AMY. Yes.

JOANNA. Well . . . I don't know. (*Beat.*)

FELICIA. Amen.

AMY. Hey, have you guys been rehearsing my script?

JOANNA. Yeah.

AMY. A-plus. I'm flattered.

JOANNA. We love it.

AMY. It's a great story. Wrote itself.

JOANNA. And it's just so incredible actually being here.

AMY. Yeah, I've been trying to soak it all in. It's like every brick in this old house could tell a story. (*Beat.*) And that room . . . boy.

JOANNA. Oh, yeah. (*Beat.*) When I went in there, you know . . . I cried.

AMY. Really?

JOANNA. It was like I was overcome.

AMY *puts her hand on* JOANNA's *shoulder.*

AMY. That is *so* sensitive.

JOANNA. Well . . .

AMY. No, honestly, that is beautiful. (*She strokes* JOANNA's *hair and smiles at her.*)

FELICIA. Praise the Lord. (*She takes off the headphones, smiling.*)

AMY. Amen.

FELICIA. Amen.

NEAL, GAVIN *and* LANCE *appear from the grounds. They carry plans and papers.* NEAL *is in a hurry as he walks through the room.*

NEAL. OK. Give me two minutes while I go get those charts. (*He looks at his watch.*) Call me if the marquee guy arrives. (*He's gone.*)

GAVIN. OK. (*Beat.*) Morning everyone. Beautiful day.

AMY. Did Neal eat breakfast?

GAVIN. Hours ago.

AMY. Make sure he gets a sandwich by eleven thirty.

GAVIN. I will.

AMY. And promise me you'll stop for lunch. You know his intestinal situation.

GAVIN. We're having lunch in town, it's all arranged. Don't worry, I'll look after him.

AMY. Good.

GAVIN. You've all got plenty to do? Not bored?

JOANNA. We've been rehearsing.

GAVIN. Smashing. Which reminds me, did you ring the camera crew?

LANCE. Yes, they finish in London at midnight, so they're driving down overnight. They'll be here five a.m. at the latest.

GAVIN. Good.

LANCE. And they have to be back in town for three o'clock.

GAVIN. We'll be wrapped by ten, so that's no problem.

LANCE. They were a little bit stroppy about the early start.

GAVIN. Typical. We're paying them three times the rate and still they manage a whinge. Welcome home Gavin. Honestly, you'd think people over here would have learned the lesson of the past thirteen years. In the States, I call someone up, I say: we've got a problem. They say: great, how do we solve it? Over here, they say: cor, blimey, guv, that's a tall order, it'll cost you.

JOANNA. My father says it's got a lot better, though.

GAVIN. Of course it has. But that was just the shake-out. Sadly, there's something soft in your average Brit that stops him going all the way.

AMY. Maybe the Lord can change that.

GAVIN. Amen to that. But he may need a helping hand, and that, God willing, is part of my mission.

NEAL *hurries back in with some papers.* LANCE *goes to the windows.*

All set?

NEAL. Can't wait.

LANCE. Looks like the marquee guys have finally arrived.

NEAL. Great, let's do some business. (*He,* GAVIN *and* LANCE *go out.*)

FELICIA. Where does he get his energy?

AMY. From the Lord, where else? (*They smile.*)

RUTH *comes in in her dressing gown, holding a cup of tea.*

RUTH. Oh, good morning. (*They all 'hello', 'hi' etc.*)

AMY. Been catching up on some sleep?

RUTH. No, I suffer from insomnia. I usually spend most of the night writing. In actual fact I've had approximately two and a half hours of something only vaguely like sleep.

AMY. I know the feeling.

RUTH. One gets used to it, I suppose. (*Beat.*)

AMY. And what do you write? When you can't sleep?

RUTH. Oh, this and that. Furious letters to the newspapers, that sort of thing.

AMY. What, all night? (*Beat.*)

RUTH. No. Bits of memoirs, short stories, sometimes, like you.

AMY. No. I don't. Not any more.

RUTH. Well, that's a terrible shame. I read two of your volumes and liked them very much. (*Beat.*)

AMY. You have my stories here?

RUTH. Yes.

AMY. In this house?

RUTH. Upstairs.

AMY *is agitated.*

Why?

AMY. What must you think?

RUTH. Of what?

AMY. Nothing. (*Beat.*) Of me.

RUTH. For a start, I think you're a very good writer. Why on earth you bother with all this evangelist claptrap is beyond me. It's a criminal waste of talent.

AMY. A talent put to God's purpose is not wasted.

RUTH. Ha. I'll bet you could write that on the gravestones of a few million poor buggers.

AMY *stands.*

AMY. Excuse me.

RUTH. Ah. Sudden pressing business.

AMY. I have some things to do.

RUTH. Of course you do.

AMY. No, I really do.

RUTH. Of course you really do. (*Beat.*)

AMY. What have I done to you? (*Beat.*)

RUTH (*indicating the scripts*). Is that the script you wrote?

AMY. Yes.

RUTH. Your talent put to God's purpose?

AMY. I hope so. (*Beat.*)

RUTH *just smiles.* AMY *goes.*

RUTH. First one of the day.

FELICIA. Miss Hartstone . . .

RUTH. Hmmm. . . ?

FELICIA. Excuse me, but Mrs. Hoffman is a good Christian lady.

RUTH. I'm very happy for her.

FELICIA. Has she offended you?

RUTH. I don't know. Possibly.

FELICIA. Well, I believe you've offended her.

RUTH. That, my dear, is because I'm a crabby old cow. Especially before I've had my herbal tea. (*She sips.*)

FELICIA. Politeness doesn't cost, you know. (*Frisson. Beat.*)

RUTH. Yes. That's true. (*Beat.*)

JOANNA. Miss Hartstone, how old were you when you first wore suspenders? Oh God, that sounds stupid. I mean, when you were young, when Grace was here, you know, the film . . .

RUTH. My Dear, you've totally lost me.

J0ANNA. Sorry. We were reading a scene, you see, and we wondered what sort of clothes you wore.

RUTH. I see. Well, most definitely not suspenders. I normally wore corduroy trousers. And a sensible sweater.

FELICIA. And Grace? (*Beat.*)

RUTH. Any old thing, really. A simple dress. Sandals.

FELICIA. Do you have any photographs?

RUTH. Only from years before, in Africa.

FELICIA. That's a real shame. (*Beat.*)

RUTH. Actually, somewhere, I have the last dress she ever wore. Yes, I have it somewhere.

FELICIA. Wow, that is incredible.

JOANNA. Fantastic.

FELICIA. Do you suppose we could. . . ? No, I guess it's too personal.

RUTH. What is? (*Beat.*)

FELICIA. Could I wear it in the movie? (RUTH *smiles.*)

RUTH. Oh, no. No, I don't think so.

FELICIA. Sorry, I shouldn't have asked.

RUTH. Why on earth not?

FELICIA. I realise it would probably be too painful for you.

RUTH. Too painful?

FELICIA. Yes, I mean, your sister's dress, and her dying and everything . . .

RUTH. Oh, I see. No, the reason you couldn't possibly wear the dress is that it would be far too big for you.

FELICIA. Excuse me?

RUTH *stands.*

RUTH. Look like a tent on you. (*She goes.*)

FELICIA. Man, is she flaky, or what?

JOANNA. Grace must have been, you know, fat when she died. You're going to have put on a few pounds.

FELICIA. No way. I can't play large. That is not a possibility. I have an image.

JOANNA. Have to eat lots of cream cakes.

FELICIA. Absolutely no way. (*Beat.*)

JOANNA. If you don't let on about the corduroy trousers and the sensible sweaters, I won't tell anyone about Grace's weight problem.

FELICIA. Deal.

LANCE *comes in from the grounds.*

LANCE. Anybody seen my damn case? (*He spots it.*) Ah, there it is. (*He opens it and searches through some papers.*)

JOANNA. Busy busy busy.

LANCE. You're telling me. Still, all right for some, eh?

JOANNA. Do you mind? We've been working.

LANCE. Yeah. (*He snaps his case shut.*) This is great, isn't it? I feel really . . . (*He clenches his fist.*) . . . y'know?

FREDDY *comes in to go through the grounds.*

JOANNA. Has someone been putting something in your tea, Lance?

LANCE. No, listen, to be on the ground floor on an operation like this . . . it's unreal. I mean, this place, it's a beacon for the future. Broadcasting to the whole of Europe, giving people what they want: God and freedom. I love it. What do you say, Freddy?

FREDDY. What do I say?

LANCE. Yeah. (*Beat.*)

FREDDY. Nothing. (*Beat.*)

LANCE. Well, there'll be stacks of work when we come on stream next year. Stick around.

FREDDY. No thanks. I'd rather not see what you do. I'd rather not know.

LANCE. Well, your loss.

FREDDY. Yeah. My loss. (*Beat.*)

JOANNA. Did *you* catch those trout we had yesterday, Freddy?

FREDDY. Yes.

JOANNA. How clever. Real countryman, aren't you?

FREDDY. I suppose so.

LANCE. Funnily enough I caught some massive salmon in the States last year.

JOANNA. Do you look after everything all on your own?

FREDDY. More or less.

JOANNA. Sort of like a gamekeeper.

FREDDY. That's right.

JOANNA. Must be a heck of a job.

FREDDY. It's my life.

JOANNA. That's really romantic. Very D.H. Lawrence. You know. Lady Chatterly.

FREDDY. Miss, I may be a little shy, but I'm not stupid.

JOANNA. Didn't say you were. (*Beat.*) Any chance of showing us where the kitchen is? I feel a snack-attack coming on.

FREDDY. Sure

JOANNA. Felicia?

FELICIA. Yeah, O.K. I'll watch.

LANCE. Meanwhile, some of us will get on with some work.

FREDDY *gestures the way and they start to go.*

JOANNA. Don't strain yourself, Lance.

*The women go.* FREDDY *gives* LANCE *a look and follows them.*
LANCE *stands, case in hand.*

LANCE (*American accent*). Goddam nigger. (*He smirks, turns and
walks briskly off.*)


## Scene Four

*The drawing room, 2.30 a.m. In the semi-darkness we can just about make
out a figure in a nightdress crouched beside the drinks cabinet. Pause.* RUTH
*comes in carrying two books, a notepad, pens and a cup of tea. She puts these
on the table and brings a table lamp across and switches it on. As she does so,
the figure,* AMY, *shifts and tries to become smaller.* RUTH *pulls up a
chair and sits down.* AMY *shifts again.* RUTH *looks up, sees something
and slowly looks round to check the windows. She looks back and very slowly
and quietly opens a notebook and picks up a pen. She sits. Slight movement
from* AMY. RUTH *puts the pen down.*

RUTH. You know, I really can't concentrate terribly well with
you scuffling around down there. (*Pause.*) I say. . . ? (*Pause.*) Oh,
well, suit yourself. (*She begins packing her things up.*)

AMY. Help me.

RUTH. What? (*Pause. Softly.*) What did you say? (*She stands and
goes over to* AMY.) Mrs Hoffman? What are you doing? (*Beat.*)
Are you all right?

AMY. No.

RUTH. Whatever is the matter?

AMY *looks up. Cradled in her arms is a two-thirds-empty vodka bottle.
She's very drunk.*

Oh my good Lord . . . (*She gently takes the bottle and puts it on the
table.*) Right, let's have you up. (*She tries to help her up.* AMY
*shakes her head and waves her arms.*)

AMY. No . . .

RUTH All right. (*Beat.*) All right. Wherever you feel most
comfortable. (RUTH *goes and sits again.*) What is it? Insomnia?

Same as me? (*Beat.*) You know, if I ever for one moment allow the possiblity that there might be a God, then it's always about now. The middle of the night. Not to be able to sleep is a kind of Hell. A terrible punishment. (*Beat.*) That's why I'm not very keen on the idea of eternity. When my time comes, I'm really rather looking forward to closing my eyes and knowing that for the first time in many, many years I shall sleep. Deep, long and quiet.

*Pause. AMY slowly crawls across the floor to the table. She puts her arm up and feels for the vodka bottle. She finds it and hauls herself up onto her knees. She takes the top off the bottle and takes an incredibly long swig. She puts the bottle back and curls up.*

Good grief. (*Beat.*) Not many people know this, but my father, my sainted, light-in-the-darkness-bringing father could polish off a bottle of port before lunch. Yes, port. Horrible sickly stuff if you ask me. But there you are. (*Beat*).

*AMY takes another swig.*

This is very strange, you know. I mean, I was under the impression that you Americans always had your drinks on the rocks. (*Beat.*) No? I could get you some ice. (*She takes a sip of tea.*) Perhaps you'd like some herbal tea? (*Beat.*) I'm sorry, I'm sounding like a mother hen, aren't I? Anyway, it's your choice. If you want to crawl around on the floor at the dead of night, drunk as a lord, then that's up to you. Crawl away. (*Beat.*) It's just that I thought you asked me to help you. (*She stands and comes round to where AMY is crouching.*) This is quite a stroke of luck, really. I've got your books here. I was going to make some notes and ask you some questions tomorrow. I've always wanted to quiz a living writer.

AMY. (*Her speech is very slurred.*) 'S all fucking true.

RUTH. What?

AMY. 'S all true. It all happened.

RUTH. Ah. (*Beat.*) Yes, I was going to ask you about that. Don't misunderstand me, I wasn't shocked. (*Beat.*) Well, actually, yes I was. A bit. But it occurred to me that . . . well, that anybody who went through all, or most, or even some of what's in your books . . . then things must be very difficult for them. (*Beat.*)

AMY. Up the fucking ass. You ever been fucked up the ass? (*Beat.*)

RUTH. No. Thankfully. I've always maintained a discreet distance from men who discussed sodomy too enthusiastically. (*Beat.*) I take it you have. Been. You know. (*Beat.*) Ah yes . . . (*She picks up one of the books.*) Yes, I know the one you mean. (*Beat.*) God. That's real, is it? The video tapes and everything.

AMY. I was paid. (*Beat.*) Couldn't see my face, not at first. I knew it was me 'cause I had a fucking band aid on my big toe. Nearly tore the nail off that morning, caught it in the shower. Fucking band aid. Little smudge of blood, the top corner. My big toe. Those guys. Those fucking assholes. They were the big guys, y'know? Extra big guys. Cocks like fucking airplanes. (*Pause. She takes another swig.*) I saw the video. (*Beat.*)

RUTH. You survived, at least.

AMY. Yeah, look at me. A survivor.

RUTH. And your stories . . . some of them are beautiful.

AMY. Fuck beauty. (*Pause.*)

RUTH. Do I take it that your conversion is only temporary?

AMY. No. (*Beat.*) But it's all messed up. Sometimes, I can't help it, I just see these things. And I pray and I pray and they don't go away and it's my fault. I'm not good enough.

RUTH. That's silly. None of us is. (*Beat.*)

AMY. My sins should be forgiven. But they're not. God won't forgive me. (*She takes another huge swig and crumples up.*)

NEAL *has come in, unseen, in his pyjamas and dresing gown.*

RUTH. Then He's not half the Deity He's cracked up to be. (*She sees* NEAL.) Ah. It's your wife. I think she needs help.

NEIL *walks across to* AMY *and takes the bottle from her. He puts the top on it and returns it to the drinks cabinet. He walks back to the table and picks up one of the books. He looks at* RUTH *and drops the book back on the table. He drops to his knees, elbows on the table, hands clasped together.*

NEAL. Lord, give me strength in this hour of need. Give me strength to bring this beautiful woman back to your love and goodness, to save her from these torments, to help her live again in Jesus Christ. Thank you, Lord. Amen. (*He puts his head in his hands for a few seconds then slowly gets up.*) Ruth . . . Amy and I have a beautiful daughter, Kimmy. She'll be sixteen years old this fall. (*Beat.*) Since the day Kimmy was born, Satan has been

trying to claim her. Not a day goes by without he throws us a
new challenge. Satan has targeted our daughter, he's targeted
us, because of the strength of my mission. The power of the
message of God's love is so strong in me that the devil keeps on
coming back, trying to destroy me and my beautiful family.
(*Beat.*) Before we left on this trip, he sent a boy from Kimmy's
school to claim her. He gave her rock albums that said 'Satan
will reign forever' when you played them backwards. He tried to
seduce her, until I exorcised the Devil from his body. Then
Satan gave Kimmy nightmares, physical ailments, nosebleeds, a
skin condition. I've been fighting him through my daugher, and
now he's trying to destroy me through Amy. And I have to fight
him again.

*Pause.* RUTH *suddenly laughs.*

RUTH. Excuse me asking, but why would anybody want to play a
record backwards? What on earth could possibly be the point?
And I'm hardly surprised your daughter has nightmares after
seeing her father do a spot exorcism on one of her schoolfriends.
That's enough to make anybody a candidate for the funny farm.
(*Beat.*) Really, Reverend, you do rather seem to come at
everything the wrong way round. (*Beat*).

NEAL *picks up the books.*

NEAL. You brought these into this house. Why?

RUTH. Obviously I wanted to see what kind of writer she was.

NEAL. We sent you the script.

RUTH. Yes . . .

NEAL. So who made you bring these books here?

RUTH. Who? It was intellectual curiosity, for heaven's sake. Or
have you never heard of that? (*Pause.*) Oh, I see. Who. Yes, very
good. (*Beat.*) Well, you tell me.

NEAL. I already know. (*Beat.*)

RUTH (*she points to* AMY). So your answer to this is that I am a
stooge of Satan?!

NEAL. Yes! Satan loves a failure. And that's what you are. He
smells out people like you, failed, bitter people, to use in his
battle with the success of God's love. (*Beat.*)

RUTH. Stop blaming it all on Satan. It's you, and you bloody well
know it.

NEAL *throws his arms in the air and stands in front of her.*

NEAL. In the name of our Lord and Saviour . . .

RUTH. Oh no you don't . . .

NEAL. Jesus Christ . . .

RUTH. Not to me you don't . . .

NEAL. I bind you, Satan . . .

RUTH. That's enough . . .

NEAL. And cast you out . . .

RUTH. ENOUGH! (*She slaps his face. Pause.*) Anyone can see Satan didn't do this.

*She walks out. Pause.*

NEAL *kneels by the upright chair.* GAVIN *enters wearing his dressing gown.*

GAVIN. Neal? What's going on? What's wrong with Ruth? (*He sees* AMY.) Heavens, Amy . . . (*He goes to her.*) Are you all right? Amy? (*He's holding her.*) Neal, what's wrong with her? Neal?

NEAL. Get her onto the chair please, Gavin. (*He's suddenly very businesslike.*)

*They lift her up as* LANCE *comes in.*

GAVIN. Lance, help us here.

LANCE. What's happening?

GAVIN. Just help.

LANCE *takes over from* NEAL, *who paces slowly around.* GAVIN *and* LANCE *get* AMY *onto the chair.*

NEAL. Gavin, Lance. Brothers. (*Beat.*) Satan is among us.

LANCE. Do what?

GAVIN. Sshh.

NEAL. Through his agent, he has entered my wife and dragged her from the path of righteousness. Her faith has been poisoned, infected with sinfulness. (*Beat.*) Satan has my wife. (*Beat.*) Pray. We need the Lord here now. We need him here in this room with us. Only the Lord can bring my wife back to me. (*He drops to his knees and prays.*)

Lord, I know you're there, looking out for the welfare of your daughter, Amy, in her hour of need. Lord, give her the strength to get through this and cast Satan out of her mind for good. Bring her back to your bountiful love to live in your light for evermore. Amen.

GAVIN/LANCE } Amen.

NEAL *stands*.

NEAL. Amy, Amy, remember what the scripture says: for God so loved the world, that he gave his only begotten son, that whosoever believeth in him should not perish, but have everlasting life. For God sent not his son into the world to condemn the world; but that the world through him might be saved.

GAVIN. Lord, I don't believe you want to take Amy away from us now. We trust you to see us through this time, and to bring our beloved sister back to us. Amen.

NEAL/LANCE } Amen.

AMY *is stirring*.

NEAL. Lord, we believe in Jesus Christ. We believe that to deny him is to die in our sins. Only by believing in him can we come into your presence.

AMY'*s eyes are open, She watches* NEAL.

Lord, rekindle the fire of faith in Amy, because before Satan got a hold of her, she was burning for Jesus Christ. (*He picks up the books.*) Satan is strong, but we know the Lord is stronger. We know God loves us and forgives us our sins. Forgive these, Lord. (*He brandishes the books.*) Cast Satan out. In the name of our Saviour Jesus Christ, cast Satan out, cast him out, Lord, cast him out forever! (*He rips the books apart and throws them from him.* AMY *gasps.* NEAL *goes to her.*) Amy, your sins are not a problem for God. He can handle your sins, no matter how bad, no matter how low, God does not have a problem with that. What he cannot tolerate is when you shut him out, when you deny him, when you don't accept that he is Lord in your life. That is when he gets mighty angry. And when the Lord is angry, the heavens shake and men go mad. Do you hear me? Am I getting through?! (AMY *nods.*) Disown the Lord and you wind up in Hell. Where every breath feels like fire, every thought burns your brain, until you can't breathe or think any more. Except

you have to. You have to breathe. You have to think. And all
the time, you're on fire, your lungs, your brain, burning,
burning for all eternity. (*Beat.*) So come back to the Lord. Don't
make him angry, make him joyous in his heart. Accept that he
and only he is Lord. I tell you, I command you, in the name of
Jesus Christ, come to the Lord. Right now!

AMY *leans back in the chair and begins a low moan that slowly turns
into an incoherent babble, bizarre and chilling.  NEAL sinks to his knees,
as do GAVIN and LANCE.*

NEAL. Praise the Lord!

GAVIN. Amen!

NEAL. Speak, Lord, speak!

AMY *babbles on, slowly coming to a halt. When she's finally silent, she
opens her eyes and half smiles. NEAL throws his arms around her.*

Thank you, Lord, thank you Jesus. (*He repeats this. AMY joins in,
then GAVIN. They reach a crescendo.*) Thank you, thank you, thank
you, thank you. (*They subside. NEAL extends a hand to GAVIN.*)
Gavin, thank you. (GAVIN *takes his hand and embraces both of them,
NEAL extends a hand to LANCE.*) Lance.

LANCE *takes it self-consciously then puts his arms around them. They
stay like this for some time, then NEAL and AMY gently pull away.*

O.K. O.K. Everything's fine now. Right honey? (*She nods.*)

GAVIN. Do you need anything?

NEAL. No, we're just fine.

GAVIN. O.K. God bless. Come on, Lance.

LANCE. Goodnight.

*They go. NEAL lets go of her.*

NEAL. Amy . . . honey . . . you promised me . . . you promised me
. . . (*Beat.*) Well. O.K. We'll just have to keep a tighter grip,
that's all. (*Beat.*) We are going to beat Satan here every day.
We'll have thousands of people here coming to God. And we'll
be sending his word out to this whole continent. There's a real
craving, I can feel it. They've lost sight of their moral destiny.
But we'll bring them back to the fundamentals of the Christian
faith, and we'll create a true kingdom of God, right here. Right
here. This is where it begins. (*Beat. He puts his arm around her.*)
Believe it. The word is love.

*FADE*

**Scene Five**

*The terrace or lawn outside the drawing room, 12.00 midday, Sunday
morning.* JOANNA *is sunbathing on a sun-lounger, wearing only bikini
bottom and sunglasses. To one side is a set of garden furniture. The church
bells fade. Pause.* JOANNA's *hand goes down to a glass of orange juice on
the ground beside her. She picks it up and sips leisurely through the straw,
then puts the glass back down. Pause.* FREDDY *comes from round the front
of the house to go out into the grounds. He sees* JOANNA *and stops and
stares.* JOANNA *realises he's there and peers over her sunglasses at him.*

JOANNA. Hello.

FREDDY. Hello. (*Beat.*) You didn't make it to church, then?

JOANNA. No fear. (*Beat.*)

FREDDY. You want to be careful.

JOANNA. Hmm?

FREDDY. Too much sunlight, it's not good for you. Skin cancer.

JOANNA. Oh yeah, right. Thanks.

   LANCE *appears from the house. He's wearing baggy shorts, a gruesome
   Contra shirt, baseball cap and shades. He carries a basketball, American
   football, baseball bat and ball and two catchers' mitts.* FREDDY *starts
   off into the grounds.*

FREDDY. Looks like you bought the whole toyshop.

LANCE. What? (*He laughs mirthlessly.*) Oh, yeah. Sort of.

   FREDDY *goes.* LANCE *walks down to* JOANNA.

   Hi, Jo.

JOANNA. Hi.

   LANCE *sees she's topless and stops in his tracks.*

LANCE. What are you up to?

JOANNA. Silly question, Lance.

LANCE. Yeah, trust me. (*Beat.*) Hey, great shoot this morning.

JOANNA (*perking up*). You think so?

LANCE. You were ace. It was really moving.

JOANNA. Thanks. 'Course, I'll give it a lot more when we make
   the actual movie. Turbo-charged, you watch me.

LANCE. I will. (*Beat.*)

JOANNA. Hey, Lance . . .

LANCE. Yeah? (*He moves closer.*)

JOANNA. Listen . . . what did you think of Felicia?

LANCE. Uh, great.

*Beat.*

JOANNA. You don't think she's . . . y'know . . . a bit wooden?

LANCE. I don't know . . . I mean, what do I know about it?

JOANNA. Listen, don't get me wrong, I'm not knocking her. It's just, I don't get a lot *from* her, y'know? There's no electricity.

*Beat.*

LANCE. The thing *I* noticed . . .

JOANNA. What's that?

LANCE. She doesn't sound very English.

JOANNA. Yeah, I asked Gavin about that. He said it doesn't matter, 'cause the Yanks won't notice anyway, and everywhere else it'll be dubbed.

LANCE. What about over here?

JOANNA. Gavin says people are used to it. Apparently most people think the American accent sounds quite normal. Anyway, only the God squad'll see it. It's not as if we're talking Barry Norman.

LANCE. Right. (*Beat.*)

JOANNA. So. You looking for someone to play with?

LANCE. I just thought, maybe, a little one on one, hit a couple of flies or even whack a few homers. (*Beat.*)

JOANNA. I'll ask that question again, shall I? And perhaps I can have the answer in English.

LANCE. Got to learn the jockspeak, otherwise you look stupid.

JOANNA. Yes . . .

LANCE. It's true. You turn up at a game in the States and get it all wrong, they treat you like a total pinhead.

JOANNA. That's very friendly of them.

LANCE. It's their game, it's their privilege. Funnily enough I play every Sunday, y'know. In Regent's Park. Softball in Summer, touch-football in Winter. You should come along, a lot of girls do.

JOANNA. Not really my scene.

LANCE. And they're a great bunch of guys. Then afterwards there's this great bar in Camden where we all go to hang out and talk sports.

JOANNA. I didn't have you down as the sporty type.

LANCE. I wasn't till I moved to the States. Going to a game over there is a real experience. Comfortable seating, giant screen replays, food and drink franchises. It's a whole culture. Not like here. Here, the overpriced, soggy hot-dogs and the putrid toilets are legendary.

JOANNA. I thought that was part of the charm.

LANCE. Yeah. That's one of the problems with the Brits, isn't it? They feel shortchanged if they're not being shat on. (*Beat.*) 'Scuse my French. (*Beat.*) You ever been to the States.

JOANNA. No. I'm going in the Autumn.

LANCE. The Fall. You'll love it. The greatest country on earth. There's a brilliant story. Apparently, in some town down South, there's an old guy sitting on his porch, and he's got a can of beer in one hand and a rifle in the other and a Bible on his knee. And as people walk by, he's shouting: 'Where else in the world can a man do this?' (*He laughs.*) Brilliant. (*Beat.*)

FELICIA *comes out of the house carrying her guitar.*

FELICIA. Hi.

LANCE. Hello there.

FELICIA (*Seeing that* JOANNA'*s topless. Beat*). Joanna . . .

JOANNA. Hi.

FELICIA. Jo-*anna* . . .

JOANNA. Fel-*icia*. What? (FELICIA *is looking away.*)

FELICIA. What are you doing?

JOANNA. Soaking up some rays, obviously.

FELICIA. But . . . you're not wearing anything.

JOANNA. Not a lot, no. I find that's the best way to get a tan.

FELICIA. But it's obscene. (*Beat.*)

JOANNA. What?

FELICIA. It's not right. It's unchristian to flaunt your body.

JOANNA. I'm not flaunting it.

FELICIA. You're lying there . . . and, there's a man present.

LANCE. I'm not looking . . .

JOANNA. What am I supposed to do? If I was draped halfway up
the side of the house whistling at passers-by, then perhaps I
might be accused of flaunting myself. As it is, I'm simply lying
here minding my own business. (*Beat.*) Which is something you
might care to consider doing.

FELICIA. I'm sorry, but public nudity is obscene.

JOANNA. So don't look.

FELICIA. Joanna, your body is a temple, given to you by God.
Show disrespect for your body and you're showing disrespect for
Him. Drink and drugs and promiscuity, all these things people
do with their bodies, they hurt God. They hurt him bad. And I
mean, do you want to cause the Lord pain? Do you? It's like
someone who loves you gives you an incredible gift on your
birthday, and you take the wrapping off and go 'Hey, wow, neat
gift' and you throw it down in the dirt and trample on it. Is that
what you do to someone who loves you so much he gave you the
gift of life? (*Beat.*)

JOANNA. Christ . . . beam me up, Scotty. (*Pause.*)

FELICIA. You know, in the States people get arrested if they
appear like that in public.

JOANNA. 'In the States . . .' I'm sick of the bloody States frankly.
We're not in the States, in case you hadn't noticed. We're in
stupid old England, where it's not considered a criminal or
moral offence to want to get your tits brown. So lay off, for
Christ's sake. Stop trying to make everybody conform to your
Sunday school bloody morals.

FELICIA. There's no need to be offensive.

JOANNA. O.K. Stop calling me obscene and I'll stop being
offensive. Let me live my life my way and I promise I won't
comment again on your tedious bloody sermonising.

FELICIA *turns away and starts to strum the guitar. She begins humming a Christian song.*

Oh for crying out loud . . . (FELICIA *sings.*) Shut that bloody racket up, *please.* (*Beat.*) This really is too much. (*Beat.*) All I want is a suntan! Is that too much to ask?

FELICIA *sings.* JOANNA *gets up, furious, and collects her things together. As she's about to go,* LANCE *talks to her out of* FELICIA's *earshot.*

LANCE. We could, er, maybe go skinny dipping.(*Smiling.*) Well? (*Beat.*)

JOANNA. You complete and utter PRAT! (*She walks off into the house.*) JESUS FUCKING WEPT!

*She's gone.* FELICIA *stops playing.* LANCE *stands. Long pause.* FELICIA *turns round.*

FELICIA. What's gotten into her?

LANCE. Search me. (*Pause.*) That's a nice song.

FELICIA. Thanks. (*Beat.*) Joanna's not born again, is she?

LANCE. I don't think so, no. (*Beat.*)

FELICIA. I expected everyone who worked for Reverend Hoffman to be Christian.

LANCE. You'd have thought so, wouldn't you?

FELICIA. I mean, how are we supposed to reach the correct spiritual level if one of the cast behaves the way she just did? I'll be in the middle of a scene, a really crucial scene maybe, and I'll suddenly look at her and think: I've seen those breasts.

LANCE. I know what you mean.

FELICIA. And I can't be expected to act under those conditions.

LANCE. It's not on. (*Beat.*) I thought you were great this morning, by the way.

FELICIA. Why thank you. I was real nervous.

LANCE. It didn't show.

FELICIA. Really? That's nice of you.

LANCE. I thought Joanna was possibly a bit . . .

FELICIA. What?

LANCE. I don't know the right word. (*Beat.*) Wooden? Is that right?

FELICIA. That is absolutely right. You know, I am so pleased to hear somebody else say that.

LANCE. Maybe you should say something to the Reverend. I mean, he's the director.

FELICIA. Maybe I should. (*She picks up the other mitt.*) C'mon, pitch me one.

LANCE. I'm not much good . . .

FELICIA. Go for it. (*He throws.*)

RUTH *appears from the house and shouts.*

RUTH. Freddy! (*Beat.*) Freddy!

LANCE. Lost him?

RUTH (*giving* LANCE *a hostile look*). I doubt it. Damn, I want him to move some furniture.

LANCE. Can I help?

RUTH. No thanks. In fact, I'd rather you didn't even come into the house while you're wearing that obscenity. (*The T-shirt.*)

LANCE. It's a free country.

RUTH. Not when the United States disapproves of your elected government, it's not.

LANCE (*he smirks*). Oh, that old line, really . . .

RUTH. I beg your pardon? (*Beat. He decides to go for it.*)

LANCE. I don't suppose you've been? To Nicaragua?

RUTH No, I haven't, so what?

LANCE. So many people haven't been, but think they know what went on there. So many people. Well I've been. And I know what went on.

RUTH. And what would you have been doing there, precisely?

LANCE. I was there working for the Free World Foundation.

RUTH. Oh my God, The Oliver North Fan Club.

LANCE. Ma'am I'm just the simple follower of an unemployed Jewish carpenter from Nazareth.

RUTH Give me strengh. (*Beat.*) Please remove that T-shirt before you enter my house. And please refrain from discussing politics while you're here. (*She goes.*)

LANCE. Whatever happened to free speech?

FELICIA *has picked up her guitar.*

FELICIA. I guess Miss Hartstone's a radical or something.

LANCE. About as radical as a boiled sweet. Champagne socialist, that's what she is. She lives in this place, and she wants everybody else to vote Labour. That really makes me want to barf.

FREDDY *appears from the grounds.*

FREDDY. Did somebody call me?

FELICIA. Ruth. She wanted you to help her with the furniture.

FREDDY. Oh, yeah.

LANCE. She declined my offer of help.

FREDDY. What a surprise.

FELICIA. Would you like some juice?

FREDDY. Yeah, why not?

LANCE *is a bit put out.*

FELICIA. O.K. (*She pours him a glass and hands it to him.*)

FREDDY. Thanks.

FELICIA. You're welcome. (*Beat.*) I just wanted to say how beautiful I think Hartstone is. You must really love it here.

FREDDY. Yeah.

FELICIA. And I guess we're kind of taking it away from you.

FREDDY. Yeah. (*Beat.*)

FELICIA. Where will you go?

FREDDY. I may go to Africa.

FELICIA. Oh, wow, roots and stuff.

FREDDY. I don't really know. I've never been. I was born here.

FELICIA. Really?

FREDDY. Yeah. (*Beat.*) Right. (*He drains his glass.*) I'd better find Ruth.

FELICIA. Yeah.

*He goes. She and* LANCE *look puzzled. We hear* NEAL's *voice from offstage.*

NEAL. Where is everybody?

*He appears from round the front of the house followed by* GAVIN *and* AMY. *They are dressed for church.* AMY *wears dark glasses.*

FELICIA. Out here.

NEAL. Well, this is very pretty.

GAVIN. How agreeable. Drinks on the terrace. Lovely.

AMY *sits at the table.*

FELICIA. So how was church?

NEAL. Honey, one word: boring. Am I right or am I right? (GAVIN *smiles.*)

FELICIA. Church was *boring*?

NEAL. Like you would not believe.

GAVIN. I'm afraid that's the good old Church of England. All hush and carpet slippers.

NEAL. You don't pussyfoot around the subject of sin. You don't apologise to folks for even bringing it up. What we just experienced, that is not a living Gospel, that is living death. Heck, what in the world is wrong with these people?

AMY. I kind of liked it. It was . . . reflective.

NEAL. Honey, shiny surfaces reflect, mirrors reflect. You don't go to church to reflect. You go to praise the Lord and hear his word. You go to hear that miracles can happen. To *see* miracles happen. (*Beat.*) The only miracle this morning was that I stayed awake.

GAVIN. Neal, what you saw this morning was the past. That's why I wanted you to go. Organised religion over here has totally lost its way. It is presided over by a group of men, some of whom proudly claim not even to believe the truth of the Bible. And they don't even *know* their Bible. 'Seek ye first the Kingdom of God and His righteousness.' A pretty simple instruction, you'd think. But if you only heard the naive political rubbish waffled out today by people who pretend to be Christian leaders, you'd despair. These people no longer meet the Biblical qualifications for Christian leadership. Along with Communism, on which so many of them were so very soft, they are already in the dustbin of history.

NEAL *beams*.

NEAL. Amen. (*Beat.*) Felicia, honey, seeing as you have your guitar there, what do you say we shake off some of this Church of England dust and praise the Lord the way we know how?

FELICIA. Amen. You bet. (*She starts to play.*)

NEAL. Let's hear it for the Lord!

*When they sing, they sway and hold out their arms, occasionally raising them aloft.* FELICIA *starts the song then they all join in.*

FELICIA (*singing*). Lift up your hearts, lift up your hands, lift up your eyes to Jesus.

ALL. Trust in his word, trust in his love, trust in the hands of Jesus.

JOANNA *appears U/S in the house, still topless. She sees them and quickly pulls on her shorts and top and runs out to join them. She stands next to* GAVIN, *who smiles at her, and joins in the singing.* FELICIA *looks at* LANCE, *then at* JOANNA, *then at* LANCE *again. He smiles. They sing the chorus.*

Take him on board, for he is the Lord. The family of man is safe in his hands.


## Scene Six

*The garden, late afternoon.* FREDDY *is tying a fly at the table as* RUTH *comes out of the house, carrying a manuscript. He looks up at her then back to the fly.*

RUTH. You said you'd help me with that table earlier.

FREDDY. I couldn't find you. Do it later.

RUTH. It's done now. (*Pause. She walks across and puts the manuscript on the table.*) There. I dug it out. (*Pause.*)

FREDDY. And what are you going to do with it?

RUTH. What do you think? Send it to the publisher. The offer's still open.

FREDDY. When are you going to send it?

RUTH. Tomorrow.

FREDDY. And when are you going to tell them? (*Pause. He shakes his head.*) You really are something.

RUTH. Don't. I've had enough. I don't need any lectures.

FREDDY. You know it's wrong.

RUTH (*angry*). It is not wrong! What they're doing is wrong. What I'm trying to do is wring some benefit from a hopeless situation.

FREDDY. Stand up to them, then.

RUTH. And starve.

FREDDY. Don't make me laugh. (*Pause.*)

RUTH. Freddy, anything I can do to mess things up for Reverend Hoffman, I'll do it. The man is a virus. I've seen it before. God knows I've seen it.

FREDDY. So you shaft Hoffman, and you posthumously get to shaft your father. Well, fine, Halleluiah. But what about me? Do I figure in *any* of this?

RUTH. Of course you do. (*She touches the MS.*) *This* is for you.

FREDDY. What they do here will outlive your book. And I still won't exist. Ruth, I've lived my life as nobody. This is all I've known, this is my identity. Give them Hartstone and you give them me. (*Beat.*) Tell them now. Please.

RUTH. Freddy, virtually every penny we get from the sale will go to pay for our debts. And, it will also mean that all those people we ruined will be able to go on living in something like comfort. And we owe them that. (*Beat.*) If I tell Hoffman and Driver now . . . Well, the house was on the market for over a year. If I tell them now . . . Oh Christ. I'd be better off dead. (*Long pause.*)

FREDDY. It's just like I remember when I was young. Half a world away, people were dying. And you organised a summer school to discuss the implications. A lot of talk about alternatives. Wigwams in the upper pasture. And half a world away, where *I* should have been, people were dying. (*Beat.*) And now you're irrelevant, living proof of the uselessness of free speech. You don't even know what hope is. And your country's been colonised while you talked.

RUTH. It's your country too.

FREDDY. No.

RUTH. Freddy . . . (*Pause.*)

FREDDY. I'm going to Africa. (*Pause.*) I told you I was thinking about it. I've got a job, if I want it. An irrigation project in Kenya. (*Pause.*)

RUTH. You're leaving me.

FREDDY. I'm going home.

RUTH. This is home. (*Pause.*) Freddy, don't leave me, please.

FREDDY. I've got to.

RUTH. Why?

FREDDY. Because nobody who cares about anything can possibly live in this country any more. (*Pause.*)

RUTH. That's just . . . despair.

FREDDY. No, I'm leaving, moving on. You're staying. That's despair. (*Pause. She looks at him.*)

RUTH. I wish I could believe in God.

FREDDY *starts tying his fly again as* GAVIN *appears from the house.*

GAVIN. Ah, there you are. Isn't this just . . . idyllic? You must have been so happy here over the years. (*Beat.*) Thanks again for that splendid lunch, it really was delicious. Everything so fresh.

RUTH. Yes, we grow it all here.

GAVIN. Of course.

RUTH. I believe you're going to asphalt over the vegetable garden, though.

GAVIN. Are we?

RUTH. According to the groundplan you showed me. (*Beat.*)

GAVIN. We'll be buying in bulk, you see. What with thousands of visitors and everything, well, the vegetable garden would be a bit pointless.

RUTH. Yes, pointless.

GAVIN. I mean, I don't always like it, but we have to think in terms of business. If something doesn't pay its way or could be put to better use, then it has to go. It's tough sometimes, but hey, that's why we're in this game, to turn a buck.

FREDDY. Then God help us.

GAVIN (*chuckling*). Honestly, you two, let go. Some of us have.

FREDDY. Let go of what?

GAVIN. The old left/liberal tosh. Come on, forget it, we're all in this together. Let's make it a success. We're all Brits, after all.

RUTH. I do wish you wouldn't use that word.

GAVIN. Which word?

RUTH. Brit. It's ugly. It's a word with its head shaved and a tattoo on its forearm. I am British. Or English. I am not a stunted, monosyllabic spit of a word.

GAVIN. I'm sorry, Ruth, but Brit is what they call us in the States, so as far as I'm concerned, Brit it is. In fact, I feel quite proud to be called a Brit. You arrive at a foreign airport these days and you're greeted with respect. Not like the seventies when anybody with a British passport was a laughing stock.

RUTH. So the last thirteen years . . . we went through all that so people like you could hold their heads up in VIP lounges around the globe.

GAVIN. Britain can hold its head up in the world again. That's the lesson. You see, in the States, the first thing you learn is that with belief and hard work, anything is possible. You also learn, working nights to pay your way through Bible college as I did, that there is actually no such thing as class. You are what you are, and you either have character and ability or you don't. You are an individual, not a member of a class. Except in the U.K. Here, if it's not some scruffy Trot telling people their place, it's the snobocracy, the Oxbridge elite. (*Beat.*) When I came back to this country, I saw something I'd never realised before. I saw that what we like to think of as respect for tradition was nothing more than a reverence of the decrepit. And the great thing about
America is that it is constantly reinventing itself, it's always young and vibrant. We have to make this country more like America, so that *we* can be reinvented. (*Beat.*)

RUTH. The eternal present. Never look back. Forget the past. It sounds like hell. (*Beat.*) Anyway, Gavin, I'm glad your youthful passion wasn't for the Soviet Union. Because if it had been, and you were standing here now extolling the virtues of Mother Russia, I'd be tempted to regard you as the trained agent of a foreign power. Kim Philby in a Mickey Mouse hat. (*Beat.*)

GAVIN. It's very easy to sneer when you see a bit of enthusiasm . . .

RUTH. I'm not sneering . . .

GAVIN. Very easy for people like you. Sitting in your perfect garden on a perfect summer's day, your inherited wealth earning interest with every second that ticks off on the antique grandfather clock in the hallway.

RUTH. Now who's sneering?

FREDDY. I want to know what you think gives you the right to do what you do. Who asked you to reinvent us? What right do you have?

GAVIN. Given the last four election results, wouldn't you say the people have given us the right.

FREDDY. A minority of people.

GAVIN. A parliamentary majority.

FREDDY. Semantics.

GAVIN. Democracy.

FREDDY. Bollocks. Your only mandate comes from American big business and American foreign policy ambitions.

GAVIN. Oh, really . . .

RUTH. Tell me, why is it that with all your talk about change, about what this country needs, you never once express any sort of respect for this country or its people? You impose the American way of life on us as if we're just laboratory rats. And all for what? Because you're in this game to turn a buck. Not a pound, I notice. A buck. (*Beat.*) Nothing about this country has ever been good enough for you, has it? (*Beat.*) And you don't really give a damn, you don't care what awfulness you create, becaue you never gave a damn for us in the first place. (*Beat.*)

FREDDY. And I'm sure you know, Mr Driver, we're bankrupt. There's no inherited wealth earning any interest. What little extra Ruth ever had, she tended to give away to good causes. Libraries, mostly. And when the local school couldn't afford textbooks, she bought them some. (*He starts to go.*) And the grandfather clock hasn't worked since nineteen seventy two. (*He goes.*)

RUTH. I'm sure you'll be glad to know that thanks to me your future workforce has at least *seen* a book.

GAVIN. Not especially, no.

RUTH. I don't know why that surprises me.

GAVIN. The skills children need to learn today won't be found in books.

RUTH. Skills?! Books are about more than skills.

GAVIN. Sentimental claptrap. Another liberal hobby horse rears its ugly head. Look, literacy is only a phase in human development. As soon as more efficient forms of information technology become established, books will die out. It's already started to happen. Look at the States, Japan. Children are visual-literate now. They read comics, they watch TV, they use computers. They don't read books! There's no need.

RUTH. No need? (*Beat.*) My God . . . that is the saddest thing I have ever heard. That makes me despair. (*She is very upset. He laughs.*)

GAVIN. Really, Ruth, the world moves on.

LANCE *appears at the French windows.*

LANCE. Gavin, the clinic is on the phone.

GAVIN. Oh no, not now, please . . . (*He goes to the house and turns back to* RUTH.) Of course, there's one book that will never go out of print. Praise the Lord.

*He disappears indoors.* LANCE *hovers.*

LANCE. Lovely day. (*Beat.*) God's in his heaven, all right. (*Beat.*)

RUTH. Just go away, please.

LANCE. Sorry?

RUTH. Go away. (*Beat.*)

LANCE. Yeah, sure . . .

*He hovers a moment then goes into the house. Pause. As she is about to go,*
AMY *appears from the grounds with some picked flowers. They look at*
*each other.*

AMY. I picked these. I hope that's O.K. (RUTH *nods.*) The lilies
of the field. (*Beat.*) You O.K.?

RUTH. Mmmm. You?

AMY. I guess. (*Beat.*) I wanted to apologise . . .

RUTH. No, don't.

AMY. I should . . .

RUTH. People behaving badly has never bothered me. Anyway, I
think you have cause. It's just . . . your husband . . .

AMY. Isn't he a wonderful man? (*Beat.*)

RUTH. Is that really what you think? (*Beat.*)

AMY. I have problems. My husband understands and helps me
through them.

RUTH. You never stop to wonder whether he might not be your
biggest problem?

AMY. My biggest problem is sin.

RUTH. According to your husband.

AMY. According to God.

RUTH. They are not one and the same thing.

AMY *looks puzzled.*

Have you ever tried counselling?

AMY. No.

RUTH. Why not?

AMY. Obviously, secular counselling would be no use. Those
people don't have a message. Without Christianity as their base,
they have no hope to offer.

RUTH. According to your husband, no doubt.

AMY. Until . . . until I met Neal, I was lost. But through him, I
came to God and Jesus Christ. I was real confused, then one
morning I woke up and realised I was going to spend the rest of
time with the Lord. (*Beat.*) Oh boy. (*Beat.*) Now, when I have to
make a decision, the Lord's right there to take it for me. Like
Neal says, He's the boss, He calls in the plays.

RUTH. Yes. I see.

AMY. And until you get to know him, you don't know how kind
and loving Neal can be. (*Beat.*) Marriage can be like that, not
the way they always show it on TV and in the movies. (*Beat.*)
And when I was in the hospital, he sent me roses every day.
(*Beat.*) And . . . I can't sleep in a South-facing room. So we
never do. I don't like flying at night. So we don't. Or he lets me
take a different flight . . . (*Pause. She seems lost.*) Sometimes, it's
like my whole life is a movie. Like I've just been watching it
happen. (*Beat.*)

RUTH. I'm very sorry. (*Beat.*)

AMY. What? (*Beat.*) I picked these flowers. I hope that's O.K.
(*Beat.*)

RUTH. The lilies of the field.

AMY. Yes.

GAVIN *comes out of the house.*

GAVIN. Amy, Neal wants you. Something about the movie. He's
with Felicia in the sitting room.

AMY. O.K.

*She goes as* JOANNA *comes out of the house.*

RUTH. Excuse me. (*She starts to go.*) Oh, how's your wife?

GAVIN. She's gone into labour.

RUTH. Does that mean you'll be leaving us?

GAVIN. No.

RUTH. Oh.

GAVIN. And before you add male chauvinism to my many
crimes, this is the first birth in five for which I won't be present.

RUTH. Five?

GAVIN. Yes.

RUTH. My, what a fecund man you are. (*She goes, taking the
manuscript with her.*)

JOANNA. Sounds a bit rude: fecund.

GAVIN. It means fertile.

JOANNA. I know. (*Beat.*)

GAVIN. What are you up to?

JOANNA. Absolutely fat zero. Honestly, these people are getting me down. If it isn't Loony Lance sniffing round me every time I set foot outside my room, it's Felicia treating me like some sort of witch because I did a bit of topless sunbathing.

GAVIN. You what?

JOANNA. Oh, not you too . . .

GAVIN. Joanna, you do not sunbathe half naked around Born Again Christians.

JOANNA. Well, obviously, I know that now.

GAVIN. Have a little thought. Show some restraint.

JOANNA. What, like you? (*Beat.*)

GAVIN. You want to go to the States, don't you?

JOANNA. 'Course.

GAVIN. Well then. (*Beat.*)

JOANNA. Do you feel at all guilty? (*Pause. He stares at her. Beat. LANCE has come out of the house.*)

LANCE. Gavin, Neal's shouting for you.

GAVIN. Right.

*He goes into the house.* LANCE *circles round* JOANNA, *a strange look on his face.*

JOANNA. If you're going to creep around like some lovesick stick insect, Lance, I'm off. (*Beat.*) Come on, Lance, have a bit of dignity. (*He chuckles.*) Look, you're neither moody nor mysterious. I am seriously unimpressed.

LANCE. Two. Two mistakes. That I know of.

JOANNA. Sorry, Lance?

LANCE. You've made two mistakes, so far. (*Beat.*) Upsetting your co-star was one. I do believe that at this very minute she's pouring poison into Neal's ear. Poison to the effect that you're one very unchristian lady who prances around naked the minute our backs are turned, and ridicules the word of God, to boot. (*Beat.*) The other . . . well, how can I put this delicately? (*Beat.*) Just how long have you been fucking Gavin? (*Beat.*)

JOANNA. Oh God . . .

LANCE. Well, doesn't matter. Once is enough.

JOANNA. You've been spying . . .

LANCE. Funnily enough, yes. (*Beat.*)

JOANNA. Lance, please . . . this film means everything to me. It means I get to go to L.A. Gavin's arranged for me to see some agents. I might get a part in a soap or a mini-series. Please. It's everything I've always wanted. What option do I have if Gavin says he wants to go to bed with me? (*Beat.*) Please. It's my dream. (*Beat.*)

LANCE. You're sort of like a prostitute really, aren't you?

JOANNA. Not through choice. (*Beat.*) Please, Lance. (*Beat.*)

LANCE. Well. Having you thrown off the film wouldn't do anything for *me*. (*Beat.*) Likewise, I don't see that I have very much to gain from blowing Gavin out. I'll go further with him than without him. So. (*Beat.*)

JOANNA. You won't say anything? (*Beat.*)

LANCE. No. (*Beat.*)

JOANNA. Oh, Lance. (*She hugs him.*) Thank you. You've saved my life.

LANCE. Yes. I have. However. (*Beat.*) There has to be something in this for me. Charity's not exactly my thing, really. (*Beat.*) What's Gavin like? You know. Is he any good? I assume he's very missionary, but you can never tell. Eh?

JOANNA. What?

LANCE. How does he do it? Wham bam? Huffing and puffing? That's what I imagined. Oh, well, tell me later. (*Pause.*) You know down by the river, there's that old boathouse? Yes?

JOANNA. Yes

LANCE. Well, about fifty yards further on, there's a sort of shed. Go there. I'll follow you in a minute. (*Beat.*)

JOANNA. Go there now?

LANCE. Yes. And when you get there, strip. Take all your clothes off. (*Beat.*)

JOANNA. Then? (*Beat.*)

LANCE. Then . . . you stuck-up, middle class tramp, when I get there, I'm going to fuck the arse off you. O.K. (*Beat.*) Say 'O.K., Lance'. (*Beat.*)

JOANNA. O.K., Lance. (*Beat.*)

LANCE. Right. Well, off you go. (*She hesitates then slowly moves off. She turns and looks at him.*) See you in a minute! (*She goes.*) Missing you already!

*FADE*

## Scene Seven

*The garden, about 9.00 pm. Centre stage is a trestle table from which dinner has been eaten. It has a white tablecloth, candleabra and flowers as well as the remains of dinner on it. There are nine chairs round the table. Standing to one side, holding his mobile phone, is GAVIN. He smokes a cigar, looking faintly upset. LANCE comes on, a bit drunk, carrying a fresh bottle of brandy, which he waves in GAVIN's direction with a smile. GAVIN smiles back.*

LANCE. Here we are. (*He pours two brandies.*) Did you get through?

GAVIN. Yes. (*Beat.*) There's been a complication, they might have to do a Caesarean.

LANCE. Bad news.

GAVIN. Not especially. Sophie and the baby seem quite well, so . . . (LANCE *raises his glass.*) Cheers. (*They clink glasses.*)

LANCE (*indicating the table*). They certainly know how to put on a spread.

GAVIN. What, in my schooldays, we'd have called a slap-up do. (*Beat.*) Is there any sign yet of Joanna?

LANCE. Funnily enough, no.

GAVIN. As if she's not in enough trouble, silly girl. She's pushing her luck, you know. Her absence at dinner was noticed.

(*Beat.*)

LANCE. The noble savage hasn't been around either.

GAVIN. Freddy? You don't think. . . ? (*Beat.*) That's all we need.

LANCE. Quite. Still, mustn't get jealous, eh? (*Slight frisson.*)

GAVIN. You're rather keen on her, aren't you?

LANCE. She's OK.

GAVIN. You should ask her out. (LANCE *shrugs.*) It's about time you thought about settling down, you know. You're, what, twenty six?

LANCE. Twenty seven.

GAVIN. Well, there you are. The ladies won't wait forever. Settle down. Get yourself a firm loving base. (*Beat.*) Children, they're the clincher. Nothing's ever the same again once you've had children. It really is a miracle, birth. Absolute miracle. When you've seen a child being born, you can believe anything is possible; that the material world has limits that can be overcome. (*Beat.*)

LANCE. I wonder if your wife sees it that way.

GAVIN. Oh, she does. She's as happy as I am.

LANCE. No, I mean right now. Now there's a surgeon standing over her in a mask, scalpel in hand, about to slit her belly open.

GAVIN. Lance, really . . .

LANCE. I expect that's one miracle she could probably do without. (*Beat.*)

GAVIN. I feel bad enough already about not being there. Please . . .

LANCE. I've seen it done. In Nicaragua. Except it wasn't a surgeon, it was one of our guys. And it wasn't a scalpel, it was a machete. (*Beat.*)

GAVIN. What are you saying?

LANCE. I'd have thought it was pretty clear.

GAVIN. I don't believe you.

LANCE *leans forward and smiles.*

LANCE. I have photographs. (*Beat.*)

GAVIN. Are you talking about a pregnant woman?

LANCE. Yeah.

GAVIN. Dead? Alive? What?

LANCE. Half dead.

GAVIN. Half dead? Half dead is still alive.

LANCE. Not in that part of the world it isn't. (*Beat.*)

GAVIN. Is this the truth? Or are you just showing off?

LANCE (*he smirks*). It's the truth. (*Beat.*)

GAVIN. I've never seen this side of you before, Lance, A word of advice, let's not see it again, eh?

LANCE (*venomous*). Hey . . . we won. Yeah? (*Beat.*) You think we did it nice? You think we walked in with a Bible and a smile? (*Beat.*) We did whatever was thought necessary. I was there! Don't pretend you don't know. Enterprise Faith was one of the Foundation's biggest backers. (*Beat.*) Sure, our boys massacred civilians when necessary, they tortured and murdered prisoners. (*Beat.*) And *we* kept the photographs. We controlled the information because that's how you win wars. (*Long pause.*)

GAVIN. I think you should pray to God . . .

LANCE. You don't understand, do you. . . ?

GAVIN. Pray for forgiveness . . .

LANCE. It's all built on blood. Not love.

GAVIN *starts to pray.*

GAVIN. Heavenly Father, into whose care we commit our souls . . .

LANCE. Oh, shut it . . .

GAVIN. Look down with forgiveness on our unworthiness . . .

LANCE *pulls* GAVIN's *hands apart.*

LANCE. Don't include me in that. Fucking hypocrite.

*Long pause as* GAVIN *gathers himself together. He takes a sip of brandy.*

GAVIN. I don't like to have to say this to you Lance . . . I had hopes for you. I thought I saw some of me in you. I'd almost come to think of you as a son. (*Beat.*) I guess I was wrong. (*Beat.*) You realise . . . you can't go on working for me. I've no option but to let you go. You do realise that? (*Beat.*) Well. I'm very sorry.

LANCE. No need to be.

GAVIN. There is. I made an error of judgement.

LANCE. You said it.

GAVIN. It's as much my fault as yours. I take the blame.

LANCE. Like I said, no need. (*Beat.*) Nobody's going to know any of this. You're not going to tell them. And you're not going to 'let me go'. Because I'm not going to tell anybody that you've been screwing Joanna. (*Beat.*) Gavin Driver, father of four, number five about to pop, the Lord's representative here on earth. Got caught with his dick in the cookie jar. (*Beat.*) But like I said, I'm not going to tell. O.K.?

GAVIN. Do I have your word that this will never come out?

LANCE. Yes.

GAVIN. Your *word*?

LANCE. Yes. I like this work. It suits me. Not going to queer my pitch, am I? (*Beat.*)

GAVIN. I feel I want to punch you, very hard.

LANCE. I can relate to that. It's guilt.

NEAL *appears from the house.*

NEAL. Gavin, there you are. What's the news?

GAVIN. Sorry, Neal?

NEAL. Holy smoke, man, your wife. I thought you came out here to call her.

GAVIN. Oh, sorry, yes, there's been a complication. They're going to have to do a Caesarean.

NEAL. I'm sorry to hear that.

GAVIN. They were worried about the baby's heartbeat.

NEAL. Later, we'll all pray. It's in the Lord's hands, there's nothing to fear.

*From the grounds* FREDDY *and* JOANNA *appear.* JOANNA *looks upset but otherwise O.K. Neither speaks. Beat.*

GAVIN. Joanna, where the hell do you think you've been?

*She walks past him to the house.*

Joanna? (*Beat.*)

FREDDY *stops and looks quizzically at* GAVIN *and* LANCE. JOANNA's *gone in. Beat.*

Have you two been off together somewhere?

FREDDY *stares at him, then at* LANCE, *then turns and goes. Beat.*

NEAL. Lance. Maybe you could go inside, hustle everybody along.

LANCE. OK. (*He goes.*)

NEAL. He's a fine boy now. That actress. What sort of a contract do we have her on?

GAVIN. Why?

NEAL. Because we're going to have to lose her. (*Beat.*)

GAVIN. It'll cost.

NEAL. How much?

GAVIN. I'm not sure . . . somewhere in the region of six thousand.

NEAL. Dollars or sterling?

GAVIN. Sterling. (*Beat.*)

NEAL. OK. Call her agent tomorrow. And don't worry about a replacement. We'll get somebody in the States. (*Beat.*)

GAVIN. May one ask why? (*Beat.*)

NEAL. For this company to work properly, we must have the right personnel at every level. Every time. Just one person spreading doubt can infect the whole organisation. I need Christians, not backsliders. (*Beat.*) We're a happy company. And I won't tolerate anybody upsetting that.

GAVIN. What has she done that's so terrible? (*Beat.*) Come on, if you're talking about a bit of harmless sunbathing . . .

NEAL. I am not talking about anything harmless. I'm talking about deeply unchristian behaviour. I'm talking about ridiculing the Christian faith. (*Beat.*) And where was she tonight?

GAIVN. She's a young woman Neal, I can't keep her under lock and key.

NEAL. Well that's just too bad. You work for me, you have responsibilities. Being here for dinner was one of them. She struck out three times. She walks. OK?

GAVIN. I think you're being hasty.

NEAL. Gavin, you are supposed to be on my team. You're the one who told me he could handle this side of things. The Brit side. You're the one who told me what to look out for: the laziness, the lack of commitment, the slacking on the job. (*Beat.*) Now, if you're telling me that when it comes to it, you can't hack it, then I'll have to find myself somebody who can.

GAVIN. I'm not telling you that. It's just . . . oh, yes, you're right. Yes. I suppose I was being soft. (*Beat.*)

NEAL. Nothing else? (*Beat.*)

GAVIN. I'm sorry? Could you clarify that for me?

NEAL. The Devil lays traps for us all. Could be he laid one for you?

GAVIN. I'm not sure I understand . . .

NEAL. Heck, I'm only saying you might have got a little fonder of the girl than you intended. (*Beat.*)

GAVIN. My wife is, at this very moment, lying on an operating table, about to undergo a caesarian section. All I can think is that I want to be there with her. How many times today do you think I nearly got in the car and drove off to be with her? How many phone calls do you think I've made? (*Beat.*) I stayed for you. For Enterprise Faith. I put you first. (*Beat.*)

NEAL. It wasn't really necessary. You know this weekend is largely ceremonial.

GAVIN. What?! You wouldn't have lasted two minutes here with Ruth. I'm surprised, frankly, that she didn't tell you to leave after last night. Anybody else would have.

NEAL. With two million on the table?

GAVIN. You don't know her. They're perverse these people. She would get a real kick out of throwing that money right back in your face. That, for her, would be a moral gesture. (*Beat.*) I spent six months of my life setting up this deal up. Do you really think I'd chuck it all in the bin for a piece of skirt? (*Pause.*)

NEAL. Oh, Gavin. People do the strangest things. (*Beat.*) OK. Forgive me. Please. I shouldn't have doubted you.

GAVIN. I don't have to forgive you, Neal. I know what a good man you are.

LANCE *comes out of the house followed by* AMY *and* FELICIA.

OK, everyone, we're nearly ready. If you'd all like to take a seat.

AMY, FELICIA *and* LANCE *sit.* RUTH *comes out of the house, carrying the contracts and a typewritten manuscript.*

GAVIN. Ah, the guest of honour. (*He ushers* RUTH *to the centre chair at the table.*)

RUTH. First time I've ever been a guest in my own house.

GAVIN. That's it, Ruth, let's have you at the head. (*She sits.*)

NEAL. OK. Let's get on. (*He sits at the opposite end of the table to where* GAVIN *is standing.*)

GAVIN. Firstly, as you know, we're here to witness an historic moment. This building, these grounds, hold a very special meaning for us at Enterprise Faith. To be able to establish our ministry here has been a dream we have long cherished. A dream which is about to come true. (*Beat.*) Where did that dream originate? It springs, of course, from the miraculous events of forty years ago, but equally, it springs from the man who made this achievement possible. The man who so reveres the word of God that he has devoted his whole life to bringing the word to the people of the world. The man opposite me, who I am proud to call colleague, friend and mentor, the Reverend Neal Hoffman.

*He taps the table, as does* LANCE. FELICIA *claps and does a whoop. Beat.*

Neal, I know what Hartstone means to you. It's a dream I've lived with for many years. All I can say is, I'm thrilled to be here, to be able to see the fulfilment of the dream and to see a piece of God's kingdom established here on earth.

*He sits. The Enterprise Faith people clap.* NEAL, *looking very pleased, slowly gets to his feet.*

NEAL. Well . . . uh . . . I thank you. From the bottom of my heart, Gavin, I thank you. Forty years ago, a missionary family returned from Africa to Britain, their work, for the time being, done. They were a pious and energetic family. Through their calling they converted and healed many thousands. They brought light to the darkness that was that great continent, and brought many souls to Jesus Christ. On their return, they were struck with a great affliction; their elder daughter had contracted a fatal disease. Conventional medicine could do nothing for her, so the family prayed day and night. There was some relief, but in time it became clear that the Lord's will was that she should be with Him. The family trusted in God's purpose for their daughter and waited for her time to come. During this time, as her mother shows so movingly in the memoir she wrote a little later, the daughter became an inspiration to them all. Her spirit and her faith strengthened them all. Nobody was not touched by her immense courage. All were impressed by the resolution and wisdom this fifteen year old girl showed in the face of death. She was living proof that death is only the beginning of our journey to everlasting life. (*Beat.*) When her time came, the family gathered not sadly but gladly, to witness her final triumph over death. And a miracle happened. As she breathed her last in prayer, the Lord Jesus Christ appeared to them all, smiling down on his charge. And taking her hand gently, he led her soul to Heaven. (*He is moved by his telling of the story.*) When I first read that book, I made a promise. I said to myself, we will take our ministry to this miraculous place, and from there we will spread the word of God right across the globe. (*Beat.*) Well, here we are! (*The Enterprise Faith people applaud.*) Here we are, Lord! (*Beat.*) Let all our efforts be for the glory of God, that we may in time establish on this earth His one true universal kingdom!

*The Enterprise Faith people 'amen' and applaud.*

Now . . .

NEAL *motions to* GAVIN, *who gets up and starts to sread the contracts out in front of* RUTH.

GAVIN. OK, Ruth. We'd like you to sign here.

*He holds a pen out to her. Beat. She takes it. Beat.* FREDDY *comes out of the house.* RUTH *looks at him. She gently puts the pen down.*

RUTH. I hope you don't mind . . . (*She stands.*)

GAVIN. Of course not.

NEAL. Say a few words, Ruth. (*Beat.*)

RUTH. A few words . . . (*Beat.*) Yes. You're right, Freddy. I ask you to forgive me. (*Beat.*) In all the Christian vocabulary, the word which means most to me is probably the simplest, yet the most problematical. It is a word which, whenever I hear it, chimes in my heart with a force I imagine the scriptures do in yours. That word is truth. (*Beat.*) I don't pretend to know any one big truth, I leave that to the men of God. But I have always believed that the truth protects us from pain. Without the truth, we will believe anything. When we believe anything, we become victims of the cruel and the greedy. (*Beat.*) I said I don't know any one big truth. That's not strictly, er, true. The truth is: I have lied to you. And now, I just want to tell the truth. (*Beat.*) I have written a book, an autobiography. I have told the story of my family, and of my sister Grace in particular. Perhaps it would have been more honest of me to have told you this earlier, but I'm afraid I lacked the courage. Or perhaps I was just being greedy. Well. (*Beat.*) The book my mother wrote is pure fantasy from beginning to end. To begin with, our time in Africa was a miserable failure. We bribed many, we converted few. And thanks to my father's only slight grasp of matters scientific, his pioneering irrigation techniques led to many, many deaths. We didn't arrive back in England our work done, we were ordered back in disgrace. Luckily, my grandfather had a better grasp of reality than my father, and he left us Hartstone to come back to. Otherwise we would probably have starved. What an irony that would have been. (*Beat.*) My mother. . . my mother was a devoted Christian, who liked to think she had dedicated her life to God. In actual fact, she dedicated her life to a series of fantasies. She fantasised my father's greatness, she fantasised their achievements in Africa, and most of all, she fantasised my sister's death. (*Beat.*) Grace was not in the grip of a terminal illness when we returned from Africa. When we returned, she was, in fact, six months, or thereabouts, pregnant. (*Beat.*) It was too late by the time my parents found out to do anything about the baby. And believe me, they would have. Anything rather than live with the truth. Instead, we came back here, and Grace was confined, a prisoner in that tiny room upstairs. From the day we returned, my father never spoke to Grace. As far as I know, he never saw her again. (*Beat.*) She died giving birth. There was no doctor, my mother didn't believe in doctors. I think they hoped the baby would die too, but he was strong, very strong. But poor Grace died in more agony than you will ever be able to imagine. A frightened, tortured fifteen year old girl, left in unbearable pain for hours, to die. (*Beat.*) I like to think that Christ would have appeared and gently led her to heaven, but I heard her screams, and I can tell you: they came from hell. (*Beat.*) My poor dear sister. (*Beat.*) The child, of course, is my darling Freddy.

AMY *is quietly sobbing;* FELICIA *is looking urgently at* NEAL, *who is staring fixedly at* RUTH. GAVIN's *head has dropped.* LANCE *pours a drink.*

I'm sorry. My stupid mother's book . . .

AMY. WHY!?

RUTH. Because it's the truth! (*Beat.*) I'm sorry. (*Long pause.*)

NEAL. Ruth . . . you didn't sign the papers. (*Beat.*)

RUTH. I don't intend to. (*Beat.*)

GAVIN. Neal . . . don't you think we should talk?

NEAL. Not right now, Gavin, no. Please . . . Ruth. I thought we had a deal here. I've spent a lot of time, invested a lot of money. I really think you should sign.

RUTH. Are you deaf?

NEAL. Oh, I hear you fine. (*Beat.*) You want to up the price? Is that what this is all about?

RUTH. No . . .

NEAL. OK. Two point two five. (*Beat.*) Two and a half. That's the best I can do.

AMY. Neal . . . didn't you hear? What she said?

NEAL. This is business, honey.

AMY. What if it's true!?

NEAL. True? This woman doesn't know the truth. She only knows what Satan tells her.

AMY (*distraught*). But what if it's not Satan?!

NEAL. It is.

AMY. How do you know?!

NEAL. Because I know!! (*Beat.*) Felicia, be so good as to take my wife inside, will you? Thank you.

AMY. I don't want to . . .

NEAL. You're all upset . . .

AMY. But I don't want to.

NEAL. Go. Inside. Now.

   *Beat.* FELICIA *takes her arm and stands her up.*

AMY. What if it's true. . . ?

*Beat.* AMY *turns and starts to go.* FELICIA *puts her arm around her and takes her off.* RUTH *holds up the manuscript.*

RUTH. I have a publisher for this.

NEAL. I don't doubt that. (*Beat.*)

RUTH. I don't want your money. I thought I could go through with it. Take the money and run. The prevailing wisdom. Well, I can't. I don't care if I die here, poor and cold and hungry. Anything . . . anything rather than see you profit from a lie.

NEAL. I suppose you think that's principled.

RUTH. I don't know, but I damn well hope so.

JOANNA *appears from the house carrying* FREDDY*'s shotgun. She walks straight up to* LANCE *and points it at his head.*

JOANNA. You! (*They all turn.*) Get up!

GAVIN. What the devil. . . ?

JOANNA. I said get up!

LANCE (*rising, frightened*). Look, for Christ's sake . . .

GAVIN. Put that bloody thing down.

JOANNA (*to Gavin*). And you. You get up too.

NEAL. Put the gun down, young lady.

JOANNA. Oh shut your great fat face. (*She motions* GAVIN *and* LANCE *to one side.*) OK. Kneel down. Come on, kneel down, hands behind your heads. Let's do this right.

*They kneel,* GAVIN *upright,* LANCE *low and cringing.*

RUTH. What exactly are you going to do, dear?

JOANNA. I'm going to do to them what they did to me. Only I'm going to do it with this.

RUTH. You don't really want to do that.

JOANNA. No? Why don't I? Why should I have to take it all in silence?

RUTH. Freddy . . . (FREDDY *raises his hand a little.*)

LANCE. Please . . .

JOANNA. Please!? That's not what you said a few hours ago, is it? No please then. No fucking please then!

RUTH. We get the point, Joanna. Put the gun down. Please.

JOANNA (*pointing it at GAVIN*). And you . . .

RUTH. You'll hurt someone.

JOANNA. Why should I care? *They* hurt people. They don't care.

RUTH. But you're not them.

   FREDDY *walks calmly up beside* JOANNA.

FREDDY. It's OK. It can't be loaded. I keep the cartridges locked away.

   *Pause.* JOANNA *starts to laugh.* LANCE *suddenly leaps up to attack her.* FREDDY *grabs him in a headlock.*

I could break your neck.

   LANCE *struggles and* FREDDY *tightens his grip.* LANCE *squeals.*

Just don't move. (*Pause.* FREDDY *slowly relaxes his grip.*) Now. Sit.

   LANCE *slowly sits at the table.* GAVIN *is kneeling upright, his hands over his face.* RUTH, NEAL *and* LANCE *sit at the table.* FREDDY *stands over* LANCE. JOANNA *stands to one side, quietly laughing. Pause.*

RUTH. Right. Has anybody got any idea what we do now?


## Scene Eight

*The garden, 10.00 a.m. Monday morning. It is as it was, with the garden furniture back in place.* FELICIA *is sitting at the table strumming her guitar and singing. Upstage,* LANCE *carries suitcases from the house to the car.* AMY *appears.*

   'Softly and tenderly, Jesus is calling.'

AMY. Felicia? Honey? You all packed?

FELICIA. Uh huh. It's in the limo.

AMY. O.K.

   *She goes back in.* LANCE *comes for more cases as* NEAL *comes out. He comes down to* FELICIA, *puts his hand on her head and smiles.*

NEAL. That's very pretty.

FELICIA. Sir? What's going to happen now? Are you still going to make the movie?

NEAL. I doubt that. (*Beat.*) Don't worry, there'll be plenty more movies.

FELICIA. Why would Miss Hartstone make up something like that? Why?

NEAL. Too many questions, young lady. There's only one question you should ask: 'Do I love the Lord?' Answer that correctly, and you won't need to ask any more.

FELICIA. But there's . . .

NEAL. Hmm? (*Beat.*)

FELICIA. Sir.

GAVIN *comes out of the house.*

GAVIN. Well. Number five, at last.

NEAL. Gavin, that is wonderful.

GAVIN. A little girl. Seven pounds ten ounces. Mother and daughter both doing fine.

FELICIA. Congratulations.

GAVIN. Thank you.

NEAL (*he shakes* GAVIN's *hand*). You have a name for the little lady? (*Beat.*)

GAVIN. What else? Grace.

NEAL *beams and throws his arms around* GAVIN *as* FREDDY *comes up from the grounds.*

Well, it's the Lord of the Manor. Any sign of Ruth? (FREDDY *shakes his head.*) I guess she's avoiding us.

FREDDY. Probably.

NEAL. Felicia, do you think you could fetch Amy for me? I think we're just about ready to leave.

FELICIA. O.K. (*She goes.*)

NEAL. When you see Ruth . . . tell her, the manuscript, whatever she's been offered, I'll pay double. However much it is, I'll double it. O.K.?

FREDDY (*he smiles and shakes his head*). It's not about truth, is it, for you?

NEAL. Young man, it is about God's will.

FREDDY. Yeah.

NEAL. It is about those millions of people who believe on Him, whose lives are given meaning by the fact of His existence. Those people I exist to serve.

GAVIN. Praise the Lord.

FREDDY. Oh, man . . . save it.

NEAL. Never, ever, ridicule faith.

> LANCE *enters. Beat.* AMY *and* FELICIA *come out of the house.*

All set, honey?

AMY Yes. I just called Houston and left a message for Kimmy. I said I'll be home tomorrow.

NEAL. But we have to go see some more properties.

AMY. I'm going home, Neal. (*Beat.*)

NEAL. Yeah. Sure, O.K.

AMY. Fine. (*Beat.*) We'll wait in the car. (*She and* FELICIA *go.*)

NEAL. Well. A setback, that's all. We'll find another location. I have a mission, and nothing deflects me from that. It's why I was put on this earth. We have the money and we have the will. Sooner or later, God's truth will prevail. (*Beat.*) Tell Ruth from me . . . she changes her mind about selling, she has my number.

FREDDY. She won't change her mind.

NEAL. Then that is God's will. (*Beat.*) Well, let's roll.

GAVIN. I'll be with you in two seconds, Neal.

NEAL. Sure. Don't be long now. (*He goes.*)

GAVIN. Ruth's book won't hurt us. If you attack us, it only strengthens our faith and brings us more followers. The faithful will still believe, whatever. That's why they're the faithful. (*Beat.*) You can send us a bill to cover any expenses for Joanna.

FREDDY. I'll do that. (*Beat.*)

GAVIN. Right. Well, goodbye. (*He offers his hand.* FREDDY *doesn't take it.*) In two months' time, this would have been my home.

FREDDY You don't deserve it.

GAVIN (*going*). One day, Freddy . . . one day.

*He's gone. We hear the car engine start. The car pulls away. As the sound dies,* RUTH *and* JOANNA *come from the garden.* RUTH *has a basket of vegetables,* JOANNA *has a handful of herbs. They watch the car go.*

RUTH. Gone?

FREDDY. Yes.

RUTH. Thank God. Or not, as the case may be.

JOANNA. I wish I'd killed them.

RUTH. No, you mustn't wish that. (*Beat.*)

JOANNA (*taking vegetable basket from Ruth*). Shall I take those in?

RUTH. Thank you.

*JOANNA goes in.* RUTH *sits at the table.*

FREDDY. He says he'll double the price for the book.

RUTH. He would, wouldn't he?

FREDDY. And I expect he'd offer more if you pushed.

RUTH. The only thing I want from Reverend Hoffman is his presence elsewhere. Preferably in another hemisphere. (*Beat.*) Well. You got what you wanted. (*Beat.*) Are you still set on Africa?

FREDDY (*he nods*). So long as I stay here, I'll never really know who I am. (*Long pause.*)

RUTH. We'll still have to sell, you know. Only this time it'll probably be a fat property developer or some ghastly pop singer.

FREDDY. At least we beat that lot off.

RUTH. Yes. God knows why. They'll just keep coming. (*Beat.*) I wish I knew what the point of it all was. (*Beat.*) You know, when Brian, my lovely plumber, ran off . . . well, I make a joke of it now, of course . . . but I was truly heartbroken, you know. I thought I'd found real happiness, but he went. He just went. And what was the point of it? The pain, the disappointment, loss . . . (*Beat.*) Mind you, sometimes I just remember the way his lovely black hair used to brush his jawline . . . and that makes me feel nice. So it's not all been bad, I suppose. (*Beat.*)

FREDDY. I'm going in. Need anything?

RUTH. A hug. (*She stands and they gently hug. They let go and she sits again.*) Put the kettle on, will you, darling? I'm parched. (FREDDY *smiles and goes.*) Absolutely parched. (RUTH *stares out at the grounds.*)

*FADE*

**END**